CREDIT
THE CUTTING EDGE

SCOTT FRENCH

THANKS TO THE MANY PEOPLE WHO CONTRIBUTED TO THIS PROJECT.
—Scott

Published by Barricade Books Inc.
1530 Palisade Avenue
Fort Lee, NJ 07024
by arrangement with Paladin Press

Distributed by Publishers Group West
4065 Hollis
Emeryville, CA 94608

Printed in the United States of America.

Library of Congress Cataloging-in-Publication Data

French, Scott R.
    Credit: the cutting edge/Scott French.
        p.   cm.
    ISBN 0-942637-70-4 : $14.95
    1. Credit—United States. I. Title.
    HG3701.F73 1993
        332.7'0973—dc20
                                                      92-36716
                                                        CIP

0 9 8 7 6 5 4 3 2 1

CREDIT: THE CUTTING EDGE
By Scott French

DEBT COLLECTION TECHNIQUES AND TRICKS OF MONEY COLLECTION

LAWS AND LETTERS CREDIT ACTS AND DISPUTE LETTER SAMPLE

PERFECT PLASTIC

THE STORY OF CREDIT CARDS

PERFECT PLASTIC

CREDIT CARDS: AN OVERVIEW

Credit cards are by definition plastic identification devices. They simply allow the user to purchase goods or services as long as the user fulfills his contractual obligations to the card issuing company. Most credit cards with the exception of Travel & Entertainment cards are set up to allow the user not only to be billed on a periodic basis for his purchases but to issue him an automatic loan for the unpaid balance every month.

The average percentage rate for these loans is about 19%. You will note this is significantly higher than most other types of loans and is three-to four times higher than the rates offered for savings accounts at banks.

Credit cards justify their extremely high interest rates by pointing out they are the most likely lending institution to be ripped off and incur losses as they are usually an unsecured loan. Over 30% of credit card holders prepay their loans before the interest comes due, thusly negating any interest and actually costing the issuing institution money to process the bill. Credit cards are normally issued with less limitations than are many types of loans.

The first plastic money was not bank-issued cards such as Visa or Mastercharge but was store credit cards. Store credit cards are single purpose cards and are issued by many businesses. They act as a credit card with regards to billing and interest, but are only honored at the issuing institution. In most cases, for example, one can only use a Macy's card at a Macy's store or an airline card with the airline who actually issued the card. Frequently there are no fees charged for the issuance of store credit cards and they are billed as a revolving charge just as is a normal bank credit card.

These cards were originally issued not as an interest generating device but as simply a method to instill customer loyalty and increase single point sales.

Because of the high interest charged, a large number of issuers are now considering these cards to be profit generating devices in themselves.

Store credit cards are issued along the same lines as other types of loans but may be easier to procure in many instances than are general credit cards for other lines of credit. Many stores will almost automatically issue cards to customers who already possess a major credit card or two or own a card from one of their competitors. This is not universally true and some department stores especially in red-line areas may actually have tighter credit policies than do local banks.

BANK CARDS

Bank cards are cards issued by banks, savings and loans institutions and occasionally credit unions. These are mainly Mastercharge or Visa.

Master and Visa themselves do not offer cards but simply provide a central clearing area for banks who wish to issue their own cards. Banks themselves are generally the policy setters when it comes to interest rates, fees, limits, and who they will accept, not Visa or Mastercharge. The individual banks are the party to be contacted in the case of any dispute or questions on the card or billing statements.

Bank cards started in California and have spread to heights undreamed of by the original offering institutions. Originally offered simply as a way for merchants to make a credit line available to good customers, bank cards have swept into almost every area of American life. Bank cards are good for merchants because they not only allow sales to people who do not have the cash on hand, they eliminate an accounts receivable (in effect the card purchase is guaranteed by the bank and is as good as cash to the merchant) eliminating the risk involved in small businesses issuing their own cards.

Banks also take care of all the problems of credit screening, billing, statements, fees and other potential problems to a retail institution offering credit. One should note banks do not do this out of the goodness of their heart and will charge the credit card user an interest rate on unpaid bills as well as charge merchants a percentage of every sale for their services. This percentage is three to five percent on bank credit cards.

Several states actually limit their ceiling on credit card interest rates to about 17%. Banks often get around this by relocating their actual credit card processing in unregulated states.

Credit screening for credit card applications is handled in much the same methods as is normal credit scoring. Banks consider a number of factors before they decide if they will issue a card to a potential applicant or group of applicants.

Some banks will pursue an open policy and issue cards on looser specifications than other banks. This is particularly true of banks who are trying to build a customer base or have a seller-side financial situation and need to offer high interest loans in order to use up some of their cash-on-hand.

The actual list of banks wishing to issue credit cards at any given time changes radically with inside corporate decisions, the economic outlook of the country, the bank's balance sheet, changes in their marketing policy or in many cases, with the fact the bank has taken somewhat of a bath with its liberal issuing policy and has decided to tighten up the reins.

Those banks actively issuing credit cards may offer lower rates, giveaways, premiums, or other inducements to potential customers. Often they will encourage customers to open checking or savings accounts at their institution and may imply such accounts actually help with the issuance of credit cards.

Banks with an open credit policy can be found in a number of ways. One of the most logical is simply to watch the local media advertising to see which institutions seems to be actively seeking new credit card applicants.

Another method for finding open policy banks is to consult with people who have a number of major credit cards and a good credit rating. Banks rent their lists of good credit risks to other banks and lending institutions and as such the old axiom, "those who have - get" falls into play as credit card holders receive unsolicited applications for pre-approved offers of other credit cards.

Simply borrow the names of these institutions from anyone who receives such solicitations and apply yourself.

This is one of the easiest and most accurate methods of obtaining names and addresses of open policy banks.

TRAVEL AND ENTERTAINMENT CARDS

T & E cards differ from bank cards in several ways. They are primarily designed for businessmen and/or travelers and as such are accepted at hotels, restaurants, air lines, travel agencies, ship companies and occasionally large department stores.

American Express is by far the largest T & E card in the world followed by Diner's Club and Carte Blanche. These cards maintain a more elite image by charging an annual fee (anywhere from $40 - $250 a year) offering a high credit limit and such perks as purchase insurance, travel insurance, traveler's checks, emergency airport cash or emergency traveler's checks, check guarantee services and other inducements. The code scoring system for T & E cards is generally tighter than that of other types of credit cards.

A very important difference is the fact T & E cards do not allow revolving credit or finance privileges on unpaid balances. They require the entire monthly balance to be paid every month or will automatically begin bad debt collection procedures. Exceptions to this are offered by certain cards on certain items, notably air line tickets but for the most part T & E cards want their money at the beginning of every month.

How do these cards make money for the issuing companies? They tend to charge a higher than normal percentage fee to the merchant as well as generate a substantial amount of income from the yearly billing fees.

T & E companies spend large amounts of money on advertising to induce applications from upper management personnel, particularly in their gold or platinum card divisions which have a larger annual fee and in theory, offer some vestige of prestige to the user upon purchase.

As one would expect these cards with higher credit limits and various advantages are by their very nature more difficult to receive than are bank issued credit cards. Most observe a strict credit scoring system as well as maintain a minimum income base for each level of their card.

DEBIT CARDS

Debit cards are the rarest type of cards and are not actually credit cards at all but simply plastic money.

A debit card allows the merchant to immediately take possession of the funds to cover any purchase directly from the card holder's account at the issuing bank or lending institution.

Previously the paperwork and inaccuracy of such systems made this idea impractical. The widespread use of computers which instantly access and debit one's account have encouraged the issuance of such cards.

As of now the largest users of debit card systems are oil companies. The smart card (discussed elsewhere) can be used as a debit card as it carries around an actual real-time record of the money available on any particular account. ATM cards are becoming increasingly seen as debit cards. Gas stations, competing banks, and some retail establishments will accept pay-point ATM cards which immediately deduct real money from the owner's account to cover any purchases.

In effect debit cards are simply instant checks which automatically deduct the funds when the purchase is made. They have a number of advantages over paper checks in that this plastic money will automatically refuse any sale in which there are insufficient funds on hand and they require much less paperwork processing, time and hassle by the bank than do checks. Such plastic money does not generate any float as it is instantly taken from the account and the bank is not lending out money while checks clear the Federal Deposit System.

Advantages to the consumer? None, or at least few. . .

Debit cards do not create advantageous situations for honest or dishonest users and simply are another step in the direction of a cashless society.

PRESTIGIOUS PLASTIC, THE STORY OF PREMIUM BANK CARDS

The five largest bank credit cards, MasterCard, Visa, American Express, Diner's Club and Carte Blanche, are all engaged in a serious war to capture the upscale affluent consumer by promoting so-called prestigious credit cards. These include gold cards, platinum cards and other premium designations. All the big five with the exception of Diner's Club and Carte Blanche, who feel their standard card is a cut above the others and prestigious enough as it stands, are busy mailing out invitations to persons with good credit history and medium-to-high income to upgrade existing cards or to join the ranks of premium card holders.

There's little doubt that any prestige involved with flashing a gold or platinum colored credit card is primarily in the eyes of the beholder. The advantages to the issuing institution are severalfold. Holders of gold Visa and Mastercharge cards use their cards 50% more often and charge150% more than people who simply use the white card version of the same card. Card issuers also demand upfront and annual fees for premium cards.

As this is written American Express wants $65 for its gold card, $45 for its green, and an astounding $250 for their platinum card. Platinum is by invitation only and no consumer can apply for it without prior approval by American Express. Gold MasterCards and Visas have their fees set by the issuing institutions themselves and as such may vary. The average is $35 - $45 a year. Carte Blanche wants $40 a year for the privilege of charging on their plastic and Diner's Club demands $55.

About 18% of all credit card volume is produced by consumers using premium cards.

Why spend the extra to secure a premium card? Besides the illusive prestige, if any, gold Visa and MasterCards offer higher credit limits, often $5,000 to $10,000 compared to the $500 or $1,000 offered on their white cards. American Express cards do not have a preset credit limit so the main advantage they point out on the gold card is you automatically become eligible for a line of credit at an issuing bank. The concept here is you can borrow from the bank should you need to pay off your credit charge bill. This may not be the most interest efficient method of paying off the bill but it is easily available and many consumers take advantage of this situation.

Other pot sweeteners for the American Express gold card are a 24-hour service to make travel arrangements and the fact one can cash checks up to $5,000 at American Express offices worldwide. American Express also operates machines at airports and other transportation facilities which will issue American Express checks from a credit card on a 24-hour basis. A very useful side effect for stranded travelers.

If you buy transportation tickets on premium cards, most provide automatic insurance (death insurance, sometimes lost luggage insurance) with the ticket. A few even provide rental car insurance when you rent a car with a premium card. It is a good idea to see if you are duplicating services here because your other insurance policies may cover these same areas without the necessity of a premium card.

Most banks that issue premium bank cards charge a more favorable interest rate to the consumer. Usually the rate is cut one to two percent below the 18% to 20% demanded on a revolving interest on a white card. Banks can safely do this because premium card holders are already in a minimum risk group and their incidence of bad debts is lower.

Besides the deals offered by the national T & E cards, American Express, Carte Blanche and Diner's Club, each individual issuing bank can offer their own package of premiums or deal sweeteners when they issue premium Visa or MasterCards. A few banks offer such benefits as money back on hotel accommodations, bargains in travel arrangements if placed through their own travel agency, and a few actually offer cash refunds on expenses incurred while traveling, such as hotels, motels, rental cars and airline tickets. This is done to compete with the T & E cards and encourage consumers to use the bank issued card instead.

A couple advantages of this situation, the Bank of New York offers a 10% rebate on certain hotel accommodations and has a very low interest of under 16% currently. They can be reached at 800-942-1977.

Dominion Bank Shares in Virginia offers a Premiere Visa Card with a floating interest rate, which is considerably lower than the normal white cards and, as I write this, is about 11%. This card is available for an annual fee of $36 but only in Virginia and surrounding states. Dominion Bank Shares is located at Post Box 13287, Roanoake, Virginia 24041, if you are interested.

The First Interstate Bank Card of Simi Valley, California, gives a five percent refund on all travel related expenses as long as you make your arrangements through the bank's own travel agency. This travel agency has a toll-free number and this seems like a good deal for someone who spends a fair amount of time traveling.

If the various services or the prestige of owning a premium credit card seem to be in line with your needs, you might check with the issuing bank of any credit card already owned. Some banks will increase your credit rate upon request to keep you as a customer on their standard card rather than demanding you upgrade to a premium card. Most banks will not offer this service unless a customer asks after it.

In the future we expect to see expansion of periphery services such as American Express' Buyer Assurance Program which will increase or double the warranty on anything you purchase through the premium American Express Card, gold MasterCard and American Express card users can reach medical or legal help almost on a worldwide basis while traveling. Some premium cards actually offer coupons or cashback or deals to encourage spending with their cards.

PURCHASED PLASTIC: SECURED CREDIT CARDS

A few savings and loans institutions across the country (and even fewer banks) offer a unique program known as a secured credit card. To participate in a secured credit card program an applicant must meet their minimum credit requirements including a steady job, no bankruptcies in the last couple years, no history of credit card fraud or outstanding judgments against one's credit history. Then an amount of cash is deposited in an account (probably a savings account) at the institution.

The amount of cash required can range from $500 - $2,000 with $1,000 being the national average.

Once the bank has accepted your credit history and your account deposit, they will issue you a normal bank credit card. This card does not differ in any fashion from non-secured cards and there's no notation in one's credit file or credit history the card was secured by a deposit on hand.

The money you deposit in the bank will accrue interest, although traditionally it can be a point or so less than the a depositor would be able to receive at another institution. This money is frozen in the savings account while you have the card. This means the money cannot be accessed or spent even though it is technically your money and you are earning interest on it while you are in possession of the secured credit card.

Many institutions will automatically upgrade your status from secured to non-secured after a certain amount of time, such as two years, has elapsed and you have proved to be a good credit risk.

Why would they drop you from a secured status and not require funds on hand to cover your credit account? Because by their nature secured cards charge less interest than non-secured cards and can often be had for as little as five to seven percent interest on the unpaid balance. One has to realize this difference is somewhat offset by the fact they are in possession of your savings account and are making money from those funds.

The credit limit allowed on your secured card will be a percentage, usually 50% of the funds held in your frozen account. The other 50% on file is there to prevent the card user from running up debts over the credit limit allowed on the card itself.

Secured credit cards are an ideal way for someone to re-establish credit after a negative credit incident or for someone who is trying to build credit after no credit history at all.

There are few actual incentives to a secured credit card to anyone who does have a good credit history.

In order to find institutions who issue secured cards start with the local media. Many times savings and loan institutions will advertise low credit card rates which can often indicate a secured credit card program or will openly admit to the existence to such a program.

If prompt sources are not located in this fashion, simply contact S & L's in your area by phone and inquire if they offer a secured credit card program. There's no disgrace in such a phone call and it may be an opportune method to find secured programs as many institutions will have undergone changes from their original advertising.

It is also possible to contact a bank or savings and loan where you have been a customer for some time and have a good credit history and ask if they will consider issuing you one of their credit cards on a secured basis.

Sometimes this will work even if the institution is not normally in the habit of offering secured credit cards as they want to keep you as a customer and have faith in your ability to maintain payments on schedule.

We have included a list of national opportunities for secured credit cards. These institutions can be approached by sending them a check for the deposit, at least $1,000 minimum, and asking for an application in their secured program. If the institution no longer conducts this business they will return your deposit with an explanation. If they do, chances of your being approved is very good. It is wise to find a local institution for a secured program before applying to a national institution.

If money for opening the account is not available it is possible to borrow from acquaintances as one can point out their funds will be put into a savings account that is secured, insured and frozen and they will receive the interest from this account just as they would receive from having the money in another bank.

CREDIT CARD APPLICATIONS; THE GROUND RULES

A non-secured credit card application is judged much as any other non-secured loan or line of credit. Refer to our notes on credit scoring if you have any doubts before applying for a card.

RULES FOR CREDIT CARD APPLICATIONS

1. Review your credit history before submitting it to a credit card issuing institution or conversely, apply at one bank only so if you are rejected you may check your credit history and revamp it as necessary without destroying your chances at other institutions.

2. Calculate your monthly disposable income. This is what remains after bills and taxes. It should be approximately twice what your bills are every month. This ratio is necessary and observed by most banks issuing credit cards. If it is not at this level, steps should be taken to change it before applying.

3. Select the bank you will apply at carefully by determining if they have an open policy towards new credit card customers. This can be done through media monitoring, asking friends where they have received approved applications or by even calling the bank and asking what their policies are regarding credit cards.

4. Be sure you have a telephone number listed in your name. If you do not, approach the phone company and have them list your name on a friend's phone (with the friend's permission, of course). This is a minimal charge of 50 cents or $1.00 a month and provides you with a phone number of your own as far as a credit institution is

concerned. This is a necessary step for many cards.

5. Type the application and fill in all the blanks.

6. Be sure and list checking and saving accounts even if they have minimal balances. If you do not have checking and saving accounts, it is wise to open one particularly in the institution where you are applying for a credit card.

7. Don't attempt to get a huge line of credit on your first card. Limit it, pay off the bills on time, and you can raise your credit limit six months or a year later.

8. If you have immaculate credit and feel you are in a buyer's market you may want to inquire by what method the bank calculates their interest every month. The main method in use today is called the **average daily balance.** When a bank utilizes this method, they subtract payments you make from the previous balance and bill interest on the remainder. This is fair but hardly advantageous to the customer.

The best method as far as you are concerned is the **adjusted balance method.** Here interest is charged on the balance at the end of each month. Purchases made during the month are not added to the interest bearing portion of the bill until the following month.

The **previous balance method** is the least favorable to the consumer as it means interest is charged on the entire balance and does not count any payments made during the month until the beginning of the following month.

THE MORE THE MERRIER

A recent trend has been for people to increase their paper wealth and the line of credit available to them by establishing a credit history and then applying for multitudes of banks and T & E cards.

This process entails visiting different banks, filling out applications that will pass the bank's scrutiny, and applying for as many credit cards as possible. When the original application is filled out at the issuing institution, the applicant normally does not list the other cards he already holds with the exception of two or three, on which he maintains some sort of balance and good payment record.

Even though the other cards are in his possession, if his balance is 0 because he hasn't used these cards, it falls into a gray area of whether they are a liability or not and the multiple access applicant will not list the cards that don't show up on his credit report.

Anyone with reasonably good credit and time on their hands can thusly establish a potential line of credit of $30,000 - $50,000. This money is accessible by visiting the lending institutions asking for cash up to the amount of credit available on each card. This cash will be lent at the usual high interest rates prevalent in credit cards and such an extreme credit line is only beneficial to a few people in our society who have access to guaranteed low or no-risk investment schemes which produce an extremely high return in a short time.

If these schemes require an initial high cash load to execute, the multiple credit card scheme becomes feasible to generate large amounts of capital which can be repaid before the interest rates take effect. This is not an advisable scheme in most instances as any loss or unforeseen eventuality cannot only throw the credit card user into bankruptcy but can possibly bring about legal charges of fraud, when money is borrowed with no reasonable expectation of repayment.

A rare exception to this rule is someone who is already a white collar criminal or has other extenuating circumstances that lead him to believe a successful escape from his present circumstances may soon be at hand. In this hypothetical instance, the criminal would borrow suddenly on his credit cards giving him a large nest egg of flight money and then he would depart the scene.

This action will constitute another crime or series of crimes which will eventually add to his sentence when the thief is apprehended. There is really no legal set of circumstances that necessitate a person having 40 or 50 bank credit cards.

CREDIT CARDS: HIDDEN CHARGES

When assessing the cost of any credit card, there are a number of factors to consider which may not be apparent in the statistics quoted or until the fine print is read. Some banks charge no annual fee but instead charge a monthly usage fee. This fee, usually $1 or under, is charged to the user in any month he makes a purchase. This translates as a $12 annual fee if the card is used all year.

The grace period is extremely important. This is the amount of time granted by the bank for receiving total payment on any month's credit card. The unpaid balance is immediately subject to revolving finance charges from the date of posting on any bank's computer, usually based on the average daily balance. Some banks charge a late fee if they do not receive the required minimum payment by the date the bank expects it. This fee can be quite high. It may go to $20 or so for every time you are late in paying.

Pay-off fees are sometimes charged to a person who uses his cards on a convenience basis instead of charging finance charges. In essence this fee brings your payment on the card up to $25 - $50 per year even though the bank is not charging you any interest. In effect you are being penalized for paying off your debt.

Some credit cards will charge a fee if you exceed the credit limit on the card. It's possible to exceed any posted credit limit on purpose or simply by not keeping one's books straight and purchasing items under the floor limit or checking limit at a retail or mail order establishment.

Minimum payment is the money required by banks in order to avoid penalty charges and maintain your credit line. These amounts are normally five - ten percent of the outstanding balance on any cards. Balances lower than normal draw a flat rate, usually $10 as a required payment. Some banks will allow you to pay a minimum of two and one half percent of outstanding balance. While this sounds good on paper, it increases the amount of your finance charges substantially each month.

A few credit cards have zero grace periods. These are generally cards that offer a low interest rate or have no annual fee and will advertise these facets of their personality, but rarely emphasize the fact they will assess finance charges immediately. These cards are not designed for convenience users as they will be assessed finance charges even if one pays off the balance.

Variable rate cards. Some banks now offer interest rates on the revolving credit tied to the prime rate or the T-bill rate. These rates will go up and down as the market fluctuates, although they normally have a limit on their negative floors and will vary only upward from these floors. Some states themselves required a maximum rate which is tied to the federal discount rate, but these states are now far and few between.

Cash withdrawals. A few banks will charge you less financing on a cash withdrawal than they will on a purchase. One should note that cash withdrawals are charged interest from the date you withdraw the cash. There is no grace period in the case of a cash withdrawal regardless of the bank's general policy on grace periods.

A few cards have tiered rates. In these cases one is charged a lower percentage of finance on a higher balance. These cards are good for people who maintain a high monthly balance and pay minimum for slightly more than minimum payments each month.

Cash withdrawal add-ons. A few banks, even though they do not have a grace period for cash withdrawals, will add on an additional "transaction" fee, which can run as high as $20 depending on the amount of cash advanced against the credit card.

Extras. Perks, donations to worthy causes, money back, tickets, free travel arrangements, extended warranties, etc. are offered at various times by various cards to induce customers to use their banking facilities. In order to keep advantage of these, we suggest you subscribe to one of the credit card monitoring companies we've mentioned.

Always read your disclosure statement very carefully to find what your credit card company is charging you, what is free, what is an unexpected extra, and what perks may be available on any particular card. Do not rely on advertising or word of mouth to get an accurate picture of what a credit card actually costs.

NATIONALLY AVAILABLE LOW INTEREST CREDIT CARDS

The following is a list of credit cards that are available on a national wide basis and which at the time of this writing are among the more reasonable in terms of finance rates. Some are variable and some are fixed but all are in the bottom half of finance rates.

This list is by no means complete and will not remain current for any great length of time. Always check with the individual institution before applying for a card.

NATIONAL

USSA Federal Savings Bank, Bank Card Center, POB Box 21658, Tulsa, Oklahoma 74121, (800) 922-9020
Card Offered: MasterCard: Annual Fee: None; Grace Period: 25 days.

Simmons First National Bank, POB Box 6609, Pine Bluff, Arkansas 71611, (501) 541-1000
Cards Offered: MasterCard, Visa; Annual Fee: $25 one card, $21 for both (out-of-state); Grace Period: 25 days.

Union National Bank, POB Box 739, Temple, Oklahoma 73568, (800) 872-0091
Cards Offered: MasterCard, Visa; Annual Fee: $20; Grace Period: None.

Oak Brook Bank, 2021 Spring Rd. Oak Brook, Illinois 60522, (312) 571-1050
Card Offered: MasterCard Gold (two programs); Annual Fee: None or $15; Grace Period: 25 days.

Arkansas Federal Savings, 2311 Biscayne Drive, Little Rock, Akansas 72207, (501) 227-7301

Cards Offered: MasterCard, MasterCard Gold, Visa, Premier Visa; Annual Fee: $30 ($25 for bank customers) MasterCard, Visa: $45 ($40 for bank customers) MasterCard Gold, Premier Visa; Grace Period: None (30 days for bank customers).

First National Bank, 100 First National Plaza, Chicago Heights, Illinois 60411, (312) 754-3100

Cards Offered: MasterCard, Visa; Annual Fee: $15 (waived for the first year); Grace Period: 25 days.

Home Savings & Loan, 827 Grand Ave., POB Box 7390, Des Moines, Iowa 50309, (515) 243-8149

Cards Offered: MasterCard, Visa; Grace Period: 25 days.

First United Bank of Bellevue, 1902 Harlan Drive, POB 1000, Bellevue, Nebraska 68005-1000, (402) 291-2000

Card Offered: Visa; Annual Fee: None; Grace Period: None; Application fee: $10.

Western Reserve Bank of Ohio, POB Box 203, Lowellville, Ohio 44436, (216) 536-6205

Cards Offered: MasterCard, Visa; Annual Fee: $15; Grace Period: 25 days.

People's Bank, POB 637, Bridgeport, Connecticut 06601, (800) 423- 3273

Cards Offered: MasterCard, Visa; Annual Fee: $20; Grace Period: 25 days.

Republic National Bank, POB 350430, Miami, Florida 33135, (305) 441-7676

Cards Offered: MasterCard, Visa; Annual Fee: $22; Grace Period: 25 days.

Sovran Bank, POB 11125, Richmond, Virginia 23230, (804) 264-4218

Cards Offered: MasterCard, Visa; Annual Fee: $18; Grace Period: 25 days.

Empire of America--F.S.B., 15 Earhart Drive, Williamsville, NY 14221, (800) 843-2443 (nationally)

Card Offered: Visa "Light"; Annual Fee $18; Grace Period: None.

First National Bank of Cincinnati, POB 956, Cincinnati, Ohio 45201, (513) 632-2350

Card Offered: Visa; Annual Fee: $20; Grace Period: 25 days.

First Commercial Bank/Credit Card Customer Service, POB Box 1545, Memphis, Tennessee 38101, (800) 238-7555

Cards Offered: Gold MasterCard, Premier Visa; Annual Fee: $18; Grace Period: 25-30 days.

Gem Savings, Gem Plaza, Dayton, Ohio 45402, (513) 224-6700

Cards Offered: MasterCard, Visa; Annual Fee: $20 (waived the first year if used to pay off other card); Grace Period: 25 days.

Manufacturer's Bank--Wilmington, POB 15147, Wilmington, Delaware 19885-9650, (800) 346-1300

Card Offered: MasterCard; Annual Fee: None; Grace Period: None.

Mid-America Federal Savings & Loan, 1144 Dublin Road, Columbus, Ohio 43215, (614) 278-3300

Cards Offered: MasterCard, Visa; Annual Fee: $15; Grace Period: 30 days.

Marine Midland, POB 9, Buffalo, New York 14240, (800) 624-6600

Cards Offered: MasterCard, MasterCard Gold, Visa; Annual Fee: $25 MasterCard, Visa; $45 MasterCard Gold, Grace Period: 30 days.

Cardinal Federal Savings Bank, POB 6748, Cleveland, Ohio 44101, (800) 423-3236

Card Offered: MasterCard; Annual Fee: $12; Grace Period: 25 days.

AMERICA'S BEST CREDIT CARDS

In order to compile a list of America's best credit cards or for the best credit card for you personally, one must first categorize one's credit usage. Are you a convenience user wherein your bill is paid every month, thereby needing as long a grace period as possible? Are you an average user, paying your bill in full some months and at other times relying on the revolving credit? Or are you a revolving user who always maintains an outstanding balance on his card?

Once you have established what kind of credit card user you are, you must look at every potential acquisition as to the annual fee, the length of grace period, and the annual percentage rate. Depending on your paying habits, each listing will take on a stronger meaning.

The best way to use bank revolving credit cards is to actually carry two, one with no annual fee for purchases you pay in full within 25 - 30 days and another that charges the lowest possible interest rate for revolving credit. This gives you a choice of which payment plan to take advantage of to realize the lowest interest costs, depending on your financial status and need for purchases at any one particular time.

Alternately it is possible to take advantage of credit cards offered with no annual fee for the first six months or year, use them as no-fee cards and then cancel before the annual fee becomes valid, switching to another freebie card.

Because of the speed with which the credit scene changes, any list of "best" cards is only valid for a certain amount of time before it requires updating. The following list is considered America's best eight credit cards rated in all three types of use. These cards are rated by an organization known as Consumer Credit Card Rating Service, P.O. Box 5219, Ocean Park Station, Santa Monica, CA 90405, (213) 392-7720.

For an annual fee of $10 they provide a nicely put together poster and ancillary materials that detail 500 credit cards in America and rates them as to best buys in each category along with sidebar materials including any applicable perks or persuasion devices which might alter any card's worth to a particular user.

They also list size of bank credit card users, the cost of using identical cards on spending, best cards for you depending on what you spend a month, etc. This is a very worthwhile service.

They publish a professional journal known as the Nielson Report aimed at credit card issuers rather than the general population. For $10 this credit card locator is a real buy and we advise people to take advantage of it.

The following classification of America's best eight credit cards is published with permission directly from Credit Card Locator.

AMERICA's BEST CREDIT CARDS

REVOLVING CREDIT

      STANDARD CARDS - LOWER BALANCES
            Mfrs. Bank-Wilmington, Wilmington, Delaware
            Variable Rate
            13.60%
            Free
            No Grace
            Card Base 200,000
      STANDARD CARDS - HIGHER BALANCES
            People"s Bank, Bridgeport, Connecticut
            Fixed Rate
            11.50%
            Free
            25 Days Grace
            Card Base 300,000

AVERAGE USE

STANDARD CARDS
USAA Federal Savings, San Antonio, TX
Variable Rate
14.00%
Free
25 Days Grace
Card Base 800,000

CONVENTIONAL USE

STANDARD CARDS
Imperial Savings, San Diego, California
Fixed Rate
19.80%
Free
25 days Grace
Card Base 270,000

REVOLVING CREDIT

PREMIUM CARDS
Fidelity Bank & Trust, Richmond, Virginia
Variable Rate
15.90%
$24 Fee
25 Days Grace
Card Base 59,000
PREMIUM CARDS
Goldome FSB, Buffalo, New York
Variable Rate
14.50%
$30 Fee
25 Days Grace
Card Base 360,000

AVERAGE USE

PREMIUM CARDS
Colonial Nat'l Bank, Wilmington, Delaware
Variable Rate
17.90%
$20 Fee
25 Days Grace
Card Base 600,000

CONVENTIONAL USE

PREMIUM CARDS
First National of Wilmington, Wilmington, Delaware
Variable Rate
17.90%
Free
25 Days Grace
Card Base 176,000

Another organization I suggest you check out and possibly join is known as the BANKCARD HOLDERS OF AMERICA, 333 Pennyslvania Avenue S.E., Washington, D.C. 20003, (202) 543-5805. This is a non-profit organization set up to help bank card holders become informed consumers.

For a fee of $1.50 per month, which can be charged to your favorite credit card, BHA will enroll you as a member. Member benefits include: access to a buying service which allows the consumer to save 10 - 40% on major brand items, tips on saving money on business and vacation travel, and how to access a computerized service to purchase a new car and save money.

Their consumer action agency will help you when you have a problem with any retailer or financial institution. They have approximately 150,000 members and feel they can use the weight of this membership to insure fair treatment for individual members.

They also automatically register your credit cards so just one phone call will allow you to cancel any or all lost or stolen cards.

They offer low cost group insurance and possibly, most importantly, they produce a newsletter filled with consumer credit tips every two months. This includes things such as women's credit rights, credit cards for seniors, updates on various lists of banks they consider fair deals on credit and will keep you appraised of the credit situation in this country.

SECURED CARDS

Secured credit card policies are as subject to change as any other policy. The cards listed below are available as secured cards nationally as we go to print, but there's no guarantee they will remain in this category so check with them before sending money or applications.

Key Federal Savings located in the state of Delaware available by phone at (302) 454-1919 will issue Visa or MasterCard with a $500 minimum deposit and will match your deposit with a credit line. At the moment they require no annual fee, give no grace period, and their interest rate is about 22%.

American National Bank is a second card available from New York at (212) 425-8400. They require a $2,500 minimum deposit and offer a credit line equal to 95% of your deposit. Their interest rate is a variable rate and tends to be quite low. They do require a $35 annual fee and do give a 25 day grace period.

Citicorp Savings of Illinois. POB 87581, Chciago, Illinois 60680 (312) 997-5720 has secured minimum accounts of $1,000 and extend a 100% credit line. No application fee, no annual fee. Revolving finance charges averages around 20%. Savings pay five to six percent.

Butterfield Savings and Loan, 568 E. Lambert Rd., Berea, California 92621 (800) 828-6602 in California (800) 521-4748. $500 minimum savings account. They extend a 50% credit line based on deposits.

Interest on finance charges average 17% or under. Annual fee $12.

United Federal Savings, 498 Clement Street, San Francisco, California 94118, California residents only. We are including them because they have one of the most liberal "credit checks" around. Minimum deposit $1,000. 50% credit line. Very low interest charges. No annual fee.

First Mutual Savings Bank, 10430 N. E. Eighth Street, Bellevue, Washington 98004 (206) 455-7808. Washington residents only. No annual fee. $500 minimum deposit required. 50% credit line. Very low finance charges and liberal credit check.

Key Federal Savings, 210 Fifth Avenue, New York, New York 10010 (718) 768-6803. $500 minimum savings account. 100% applied to the credit line. $25 application fee. No annual fee. Fairly high (over 20%) interest charge. 5.5% interest on the savings account.

Santa Clara Savings, POB 730, Santa Clara, California 95052 (408) 243-9470. California residents only. Extremely liberal credit check. Required minimum of $1,000 to be applied to a 50% credit line. Deposits over $2,500 receive a credit line of 100%. No yearly fee. Low interest.

Heritage Exchange, 301 Plymouth Drive N.E., Dalton, Georgia 30720. This is a group of consumers who utilize their lump status to provide access to various financial services including business loans, signature loans, etc. There is a $10 joining fee to receive their package of "customer services" and they include a secured credit card application when you join.

National Home Shoppers, National Credit Center, Inc., 411 Deese Road, Ozark, Alabama 36361 (205) 774-3394. National Home Shoppers sell consumer items including: answering machines, calculators, cookware, stereos, radar detectors, etc., through mail marketing. They offer instant credit to anyone with no credit check.

An interesting point is they charge 0% interest on revolving accounts and they only bill five percent on the unpaid balance. You pay them directly (after paying a $25 set-up charge) and you receive the items UPS or through the mail then you pay a minimum of five percent each month until the item is paid off without finance charges.

National Home Shoppers will give your credit history upon request to any organization that you specify. You can use them as a credit reference when applying for credit cards or other types of credit.

CHARGE BACKS, REJECTS AND WITHHOLDING PAYMENT

Under the Fair Credit Billing Act as well as a number of applicable laws, a number of situations exist wherein the credit card user is not liable for payment of goods or services or is legally entitled to a refund for items on his billing account.

A user is legally entitled to not pay any credit card purchase for which he does not receive merchandise, did not order merchandise, or if the merchandise is not up to the standards he expected or were advertised.

In order to deny payment for an item certain conditions must be true: A. The charge in question must exceed $50. B. The user must have made an effort to resolve the dispute directly with the merchant. C. The user must make the institution responsible for the credit card aware of this dispute. This notification must be in writing (certified letter). D. The merchant in question must be located within 100 miles of the card user's residence or billing address.

If the user discovers what he believes to be an error on the monthly billing statement, by law he must notify the credit card company in writing within 60 days the above statement was mailed.

By law they must acknowledge their awareness of this dispute in writing within the following 30 days.

Once the dispute has been officially recognized, the institution which issued the card must either agree with the user's side of the dispute, thus nullifying any payment, or must send written details as to why the payment must be made. It is important to realize the impetus is on the issuer to document any request for payment and substantiate any claims they make.

While the dispute is active the amount in question is _not_ paid. The consumer holds all monies until the dispute is resolved.

No negative credit report or collection procedures can be instituted until the dispute is resolved. Such resolution must take place within 90 days.

The above details a non-payment or withholding of payment on the consumer's part usually due to an error in the billing but sometimes caused by defective merchandise or false sales claims on the part of the merchant or retailer.

Rejects and/or charge backs occur between the retailer and the bank that collects the money on the Visa or MasterCard account or Visa or MasterCard clearing house. Rejects occur when there is an error in billing or mistake in the paperwork between the merchant and the bank and is usually caught by the bank's procedures. Charge backs occur when the bank actually takes money from the merchant's account or their next deposit to repay the consumer as a result of one or more number of disputed facts.

In either event, money is refunded directly to the consumer or credited to the consumer's credit card account.

These facets of the credit card business exist to maintain a high level of integrity in a field that could otherwise be somewhat ambiguous. Many merchants do not agree with the number or validity of the reasons for rejects or charge backs but must succumb to the will of the government or the banking institution. To be fair it should be pointed out the use of the charge back system does incur a certain amount of fraud and as such costs the merchant or retailer money when the bank debits the consumer's account even though the service or item in question may have been delivered satisfactorily.

Any large service or retail organization must observe the rules we've included in this book and establish an enforceable security policy to prevent major losses.

A list of reasons for withholding payment for rejects and/or charge backs would include:

Ineligible Copy - results from a felt tip pen being used on a manual credit card form.

Disputed Charge - a claim is entered that the object in question was never ordered. The user may demand to see his signature on an original card slip. Obviously if this is a phone or other direct mail order this may be imposs-iible to provide.

Ineligible Transaction - similar to an ineligible copy that the numbers or signatures are not clear enough on the processing form.

Negative Verification - when a retail sales person did not use the issued hot list and a card which has exceeded its limit or reported stolen has been used for the transaction.

Non-card - in this instance the numbers indicate a card was not ever issued to this account. The card may be altered, counterfeit or otherwise suspect.

Imprint missing - means the merchant's identification imprint is not on the order.

No Motor Vehicle Identification - selectively used by banks where there has been trouble in the past to enforce an addition backup ID with charge slips. Not normally used.

Unauthorized Signature - easy area for fraud. The user claims the signature on the card billing is not his.

Non-receipt of the Item - another major area where problems. occur. The user claims the item was never delivered. There are specific ways to counteract this we've covered elsewhere.

Smeared or Missing Account Number - an unreadable entry on the charge slip.

Charge Exceeds Floor Limit - the retailer or merchant did not get a verbal authorization number when the charge exceeded the arbitrary limit set by the issuing institution.

Signature Missing.

Duplicate Processing - the same order has been or appears to have been processed more than once.

Unauthorized User - the card was used by someone who did not have permission. The owner is not legally responsible.

Processing Error - covers a wide variety of sins where numbers do not match.

Ineligible Charge Card - covers altered, counterfeit, fraudulent or white plastic credit cards.

Split Sale - a sale is divided into more than one part and the sequentially numbered transactions are suspicious because they could be duplicate charges.

Account Number in Error - account number may have been entered on the wrong line on the charge slip.

Non-matching Account Number - the bank cannot locate the cards account number in its file. It is possible the number may be in error.

Expired Card.

Poor Description - it is not clear what goods or service were purchased and the customer is probably disputing it. These disputes are common on telephone orders that may be unauthorized or placed by children or others who have no legal right to do so.

Overdue Settlement - the order was returned or otherwise the dispute was settled with the retailer who did not put the charge back through himself.

Credit not Received - Similar to the above. The person owning the card claims he was due credit and has never received it on any transaction.

Error in Addition.

Late Deposit - the merchant fails to deposit the charge in the arbitrary time limit, usually three days.

Requested Original Not Received - in a dispute the merchant must produce the original charge slip used in any transaction.

Inquiry Has Aged - a dispute or inquiry was not answered within the legal time limit and is being denied.

Check Digit Invalid - the numbers on the card did not add up to the parity or check digit included in the card number.

Merchant Information Invalid - the merchant has submitted a deposit for XX amount of dollars but has not submitted documentation to validate the entire deposit.

Decline of Approval - the card has exceeded its credit limit and the bank will not pay.

Invalid Authorization Date - can be an error by the merchant or a deliberate piece of misinformation by the person ordering.

Record Out of Sequence - the numbers on the charge slips are skipping around.

Lost or Stolen Card.

Authorization Referral - a catch-all phrase meaning the merchant must contact the bank to discuss the particular problem.

The above list in not all inclusive but does illustrate a large number of reasons for debits to a merchant's account either caused by honest errors, oversights, or deliberate attempts at fraud.

CHARGE BACKS AND REJECTS - FROM THE CONSUMER'S VIEWPOINT

A consumer gets a credit card bill that reflects charges on an item he has already paid off or a tourist rents a car on a credit card only to have the car break down and force him to use alternate methods of transportation. The rental company responds with another car but does not offer to pay for the hassle and expense the renter incurred.

A man buys a tape recorder which requires two trips back to the merchant to get it in working order. On the third breakdown, the man decides he doesn't wish to have the machine any more as it obviously is of poor workmanship.

What do these items have in common? In the above cases, the real life consumers received money back in the form of credit on their charge accounts even though the merchants did not agree with the consumer's point of view. This is the magic of charge backs as dictated under the 1974 Truth and Lending Act.

Prior to that time, any item purchased or rented on a card and found to be unsatisfactory required a settlement strictly between you and the merchant. The issuing bank took no part in this settlement, demanded their payment be made regardless of your efforts, threatened to and did put black marks against the consumer's credit rating if the bill was not paid in full while the dispute was going on.

The Fair Credit Billing Act, an amendment to the Truth and Lending Act, now protects consumers by allowing them to enlist the bank's aid in a dispute regarding billing errors or unsatisfactory merchandise or services. This gives the consumer great leverage in resolving disputes as long as he plays by the rules so established.

39

If you find an error on your bill from a bank or a T & E card, you have 60 days in which to inform the issuer in writing of the error. Then you can withhold payment on the disputed portion of the bill. In effect this is a reject not a charge back as you have never paid the bill.

The credit card issuer has to get back to you with a decision about whether the reject is to be allowed within 90 days or two billing cycles, whichever comes first. In the case of rejects, and as we will see in a moment, charge backs, the law and the legal process favors the consumer in theory and in fact. This is true because you are actually enlisting the help of a giant institution - the card issuing institution, to resolve the debate. Remember they are not out any money as they withhold the payment to the merchant or retailer with whom you are having the problem.

This puts the impetus on the merchant to prove his side of the story. If he fails to respond within the time period or if the bank finds his response to be in error or does not fulfill one of their points, they will side with you in the matter and not pay the bill. You are not obligated to pay the interest charge on the disputed portion (unless the ruling goes against you) nor can any notation or negative information be entered in your credit report.

In real life many of the companies including Visa and Mastercharge establish a more liberal policy than that dictated by the law. Both companies say it doesn't matter if you've already paid the bill with the disputed charge on it before you discover the error. They will still allow you to withhold payment on the next billing cycle or will credit you with the money while the dispute is resolved. Many times they will go beyond the legal 60 day limit and in almost all cases, favor the consumer rather than the merchant.

In the case of Visa and Mastercharge it is up to the individual bank to decide under what guidelines they will honor a reject or charge back. Some banks have been known to pay off disputed errors a full year after the error was committed, clearly favoring the consumer instead of sticking to the letter of the law.

The charge back is a slightly different situation. A charge back results because you have a dispute over the actual merchandise or service paid for on the card rather than the bill itself. Charge backs have specific rules just as rejects do. To take advantage of the charge back clause under the Fair Credit Billing Act, you must contact the merchant with whom you have the dispute and try to resolve it as you wish to see it resolved with the merchant.

There is no requirement this be done formally or in writing. A phone call will suffice with all five of the major credit card issuing agencies we've discussed.

Once you have established the boundaries of the dispute and the retailer or merchant refuses to give you satisfaction, the next step is to write the consumer service department of the credit card issuer. That is the bank that issued the credit card. Note: don't include this with your payment. This goes to a separate department and can easily be lost if sent to the payment clerk instead of being routed to the customer service department.

In this letter state the essentials including your name, address, credit card number, what your side of the dispute is including the fact you have attempted to get a resolution from the merchant and state the amount you are withholding from your credit card payment, assuming you have not already paid the bill. State you wish to request a charge back as given in the rules of the Fair Credit Billing Act.

This means you should not pay for any problem purchases. Instead follow the above directions. If you have already paid the full bill before the problem arose, your credit card issuer should deduct the disputed amount from the next statement you receive.

By law the special rules under the Act only apply if the purchase was more than $50 and occurred within 100 miles of your home.

In reality, all the major companies will listen to a charge back request without concern of when you paid the bill, the amount of the purchase or where the original disputed purchase took place. Don't be shy about asking for charge backs.

The issuing bank forwards the charge back to the bank where the merchant deposited his original credit card receipt. Again, if this merchant doesn't protest you automatically win. Otherwise the weight of the dispute shifts to the merchant who has to convince his bank that he is in the right and you are in the wrong. If the bank decides the merchant is correct and you are wrong, they will re-issue the bill.

This does not settle the matter. Your bank will take another look at the dispute and decide if they wish to support the merchant's bank or support you. Oddly enough most banks will support the consumer rather than the merchant or the other bank.

Should this happen and the merchant's bank either decides to go along with the decision giving you back the money or it can take the dispute to an arbitration board, provided by both Visa and MasterCard clearing organizations. This arbitration does not concern you. It is completely between your bank and the merchant's bank. You will not even be notified of the process.

If you feel your issuing bank has been unfair in resolving your charge back request, write a letter to the Division of Consumer and Community Affairs, Board of Governors, Federal Reserve System, 20th and C Sts., N.W., Washington, D. C. 20551. This federal agency will reply to you within 15 days with an indication of action to be taken. No 60 day time limit exists on a dispute for poor goods or when you demand a refund for the merchandise. This is strictly for purposes of billing error only.

American Express is the only company which will honor charge back requests over the phone. In fact they prefer it that way. Calling the American Express Customer Service Department, causes an automatic charge back on the disputed amount and will cause the process of arbritration with the merchant to be in your name.

Good reasons for invoking the Special Rules charge backs include: merchandise that breaks down or doesn't live up to its reasonable claim, merchandise that's not what you had anticipated or what you ordered, poor service (this can include lost luggage on an airline), mail order disputes or non-receipt of goods, billing errors and a number of other more customized disputes.

Who wins? The national percentage of consumers who request a charge back and receive at least partial satisfaction or the entire disputed amount back, varies between 75% - 80%.

American Express processes a couple thousand charge backs every month and as with bank credit card issuers, if there is any question at all about the dispute, that is if the merchant cannot prove his side of the story to the complete satisfaction to the consumer service department, they will grant the charge back.

Winning the charge back dispute does not end the affair. If the merchant wishes to followup he can still institute civil proceedings and sue you in Small Claims Court. For the most part, the law favors the consumer and gives you protection against bad workmanship, faulty merchandise, and bad service. Even if the merchant or service supplier has a written no refund-no warranty guarantee you can still get a charge back if you prove your rights have been violated.

It is imperative to charge purchases if you feel a dispute may arise later.

SMART CARD

Within the next few years, possibly less, we are going to see the replacement of the plastic credit card as we know it today, with a genius device colloquially known as the "smart card".

This card is being made by IBM at the moment and tested in numerous places in the United States and several foreign countries. In fact, in France this type of card is already replacing many of the credit cards and bank cards in service.

The difference between the smart card and the normal credit card is simply a silicon chip embedded in the lower right hand corner of the card and eight small electrical contacts imprinted on the surface of the card. This chip holds thousands of bits of information. It is a memory chip much like a ram chip in a regular computer. Along with the magnetic strip on the card, which only holds a few bits of information, and with the PIN (Personal Identification Number) system, the smart card accomplishes many things a normal credit card cannot.

For instance, the chip can be imprinted with a credit limit and every time a purchase is made, it is subtracted from the amount of credit available on the card itself. Thereby, it keeps a running, up to the minute total of credit line still available and prevents any over-run on the card.

This card will automatically record how its been used, what it has been used to purchase, along with often it's been used, giving a complete financial analysis of the user's habits. This information you can bet, will find its way into computers and onto mailing lists and also, one would have to suspect, become available to the IRS, making it much easier to follow any card's transactions.

The smart card can also be programmed to take a PIN number that can be changed at random times for higher security. It can have limitations as to what can and cannot be done with the card. That is, if cash can be extracted, certain items can be purchased or not, and soon. One smart card can replace many dumb cards.

To operate this card, the owner inserts it in an automated teller machine and the card communicates with the machine, telling it how much money is left and what the owner can and cannot do with it.

If by some reason the card has been altered, tampered with, the credit line exceeded or other unusual circumstances have occurred, the card will tell the machine to capture and hold the card and/or alert security personnel to the use of the card.

The logic chip in the card contains the list of all transactions for which the card has been used making it nearly impossible to deny card use and clearing up any question of returning money or charge backs. It can also include telephone numbers and various procedures detailed by the issuer to automatically check to ascertain that the card is indeed still good, still valid, and has lived beyond its cancellation date.

This sounds complicated but it is really no more involved than is a calculator. The process requires one chip and depending on the type of chip, can even get away without using a power supply as it is reprogrammed every time it is inserted into a machine to complete a transaction.

Right now the card is being tested as a credit card, an ATM card, a check guarantee card and a stock transaction card in parts of the United States. The cards themselves cost only $2.80 more than the standard credit card from IBM and we can expect this price to go down in the future as manufacturing technology catches up with the demand.

It is safe to assume that this card will replace standard ATM cards, credit cards, store cards and even telephone service cards within the next ten years. The days of credit card fraud may be coming to a rather abrupt end as the technology required to misuse the smart card is significantly greater than the technology required to commit fraud on today's dumb white plastic. Much of the human element is removed.

The problem with the smart card is that it leads us towards a cashless society where every transaction is immediately open and available to anyone with access to the computers where the information is stored. One's life also becomes a complete open book to any government agency, credit agency or snooper that can get into the computer.

The advantages of the card from the merchant's standpoint are: less fraudulent use, fewer problems in tracing cards or dealing with stolen cards, no problem with cards exceeding their credit limit or being used passed expiration dates, or after they have been cancelled. The new card keeps the transactions instantly up to date creating no float or unused cash in accounts.

Coming soon to a theater near you.

REPAIRING BROKEN CREDIT

HOW AGENCIES, ATTORNEYS AND COUNSELORS FIX CREDIT RATINGS

REPAIRING BROKEN CREDIT

In order to fully understand the effect credit or the lack of credit can have on one's life, it is important to realize how this information is assimilated and dispatched. Credit is a very broad term and often covers more than one's ability to pay one's bills.

To grasp the true scope of the credit reporting business, one should realize that not only is a background credit check assembled when one applies for a loan, it is often used in other circumstances, such as by employers to screen prospective job applicants, detective agencies to get background checks for one reason or another, or in some cases even potential spouses who wish to know the "Dun and Bradstreet" on their intended.

The actual amount of information obtainable in a credit report varies as much as the quality of said information can vary.

Credit reports are furnished by companies known as credit bureaus. There are literally several hundred credit bureaus in the United States alone. The total force of "agents" involved in preparing and disseminating this information is higher than the number of actual intelligence agents who work for most countries in the United Nations. Unfortunately, the quality of their work may not be nearly as meticulous as proper intelligence agents.

Credit bureaus assemble information on individuals and then pass this information on to their subscribers. Subscribers are normally businesses such as banks, insurance companies, department stores, hospitals, credit unions, etc. These organizations pay a set fee to belong to the credit bureau and in some cases may pay a slight additional fee each time a credit report is run.

For years there was no legal recourse or guarantee of the accuracy of the information given out by credit bureaus, even though said information could and often did, change people's lives irrevocably. This has changed somewhat due to the Fair Credit Reporting Act of 1971 (see the copy enclosed elsewhere) which imports some safeguards as to the type and actual validity of the information contained and passed on by credit agencies.

How do credit bureaus get their information? Most depend solely on input from businesses which subscribe to their services. These businesses, particularly banks and lending institutions, turn in information on anyone within their realm and are usually given an incentive from the credit bureau in the form of reduced rates or paybacks for every report they turn in. In turn, this material is added to the existing report on an individual, or in some cases, a new report is then initiated.

It is a common mistake to think credit bureaus contain accurate or even the same information on any individual. The reports are often incomplete and may be inaccurate. They will differ from one bureau to another.

The largest credit bureaus in this country, which we've listed, tend to comprise the major source of credit information for the larger banks and corporations in America, but many small credit bureaus still fill a niche in the credit reporting industry. If one compares one's credit reports from various credit bureaus or agencies, one may find that information is not complete even when taken in whole nor is it necessarily correct. Each agency may in actuality give a different report on the consumer than his brothers.

Besides producing a credit report some credit bureaus actually score credit reports. A potential creditor will apply a statistical model to a credit agent's report or the credit bureau may do this for the subscriber. This statistical report has been compiled by a specialized company which has taken a mass of individual consumer cases and assessed a probability of success to each case. This means they have taken bad debts, good debts, late payments, salary ranges, ownership of property, debts versus

49

income, and so on and compiled a statistical scoring system that in theory at least, shows a potential lender what is the applicant's probability of paying back any loans is going to be.

Because of the Equal Opportunity Credit Act (ECOA) discrimination is prohibited in lending on grounds of race, sex, or martial status. Age is also not to be scored in such a way that older people are discriminated against.

The idea of applying a credit scoring system to a report is to allow the manager of any lending institution to assess a theoretical probability of the success of the loan. The scoring system presents a point average of each application and this average can then be compared to the probability charts provided by the system. Normally there is a good, a bad, and a middle area in which decisions are left up to each individual institution, although it is safe to say that most institutions will not lend money on any point score that falls into the negative range or at least falls too far into the negative range.

It should be noted that even within institutions such as banks, the required point score may vary from loan to loan or from time to time as the lending policy of the bank and the available cash for loans changes. Even if the scoring system remains the same, the acceptable threshold may vary from time to time allowing the institution to dip into the so-called middle ground and grant loans that may not otherwise be deemed acceptable.

For this reason it is often advantageous to the consumer to apply at a number of separate institutions for loans or credit. He may find if he falls into the middle area some institutions may not, at that particular point in time, wish to grant him credit while other institutions may be more likely to do so.

It can also be said that even though the Equal Opportunity Credit Act does apply to the scoring systems, many of the systems have built in bias factors where women, single people, or minorities are found to score lower than white yuppies, white upper-middle class professionals, even though they are not actively discriminated against. This built in bias is much the same as is contained in some intelligence quotient tests where certain questions are easier for people with a middle class or upper-middle class background to answer correctly than they are for minorities.

According to the FC act, women cannot be discriminated against in any form. While this sounds great on the surface, many scoring systems automatically rate women much lower than men because of the automatic bias our society puts on women; i.e., they tend not to have as many bank accounts, credit cards, houses in their name or may not be making as much money as men in a similar group. This is especially true if the women aren't married or have been married and are recently divorced and suddenly their credit history is only that of their husband's instead of themselves.

One should note that a number of speciality banks and companies have risen in the last few years to take advantage of this situation by going out of their way to lend money to women and/or minorities. If you are applying for credit, look around for an institution that will favor your social and economic status.

Each individual scoring system is different and most scoring systems have a built-in life span, normally two to four years. After that the system will be remolded to incorporate new factors in society and the lending atmosphere of the time. Each separate scoring system from department stores and oil companies to banks has its own profile and while you may fall near the middle or the bottom of one scoring system, your position may actually rate much higher in another scoring system.

In order to understand the factors that go into a scoring system and the factors that determine how your credit history is rated by these institutions, please go over our theoretical rule chart listing credit factors. At the same time realize this scoring sheet will be read along with the credit report that details your actual credit and payment history. Even if you look stable on paper an incomplete or negative credit report will still queer most credit applications.

Before we get into the process of repairing broken credit, let's look a little more at the reporting agencies themselves.

In the United States there are five main credit bureaus: TRW, CBI, Associated Credit, Trans Union and Shelton. The odds are you will have a brush with at least one of these bureaus every time your apply for a major loan or a job with a major corporation. These bureaus along with their little brothers which we've not named, are credit reporting agencies. They simply rehash and relay the credit information that is provided to them by their subscribers every time a credit report is required.

In certain instances these same agencies become investigative credit agencies. This means for a higher fee they will not only report your actual credit history on file, but they will compile an investigative report from an agency much like a private detective, although normally using lower paid and less trained investigators. This investigative agency many contact your friends, employers, neighbors, or people mentioned as references, and compile a file information about you, including and not limited to, such items as if you are a good housekeeper, have domestic problems, drink, have a bad driving record, a criminal background, hang around with people they might consider disreputable, gamble or other habits that might influence a potential lender or employer.

The "field reps" involved in compiling these reports are under pressure to average 25 - 30 such detailed investigative reports each and every day on the job. You can imagine the amount of effort that is put into each individual and the possibility of error or hearsay to enter such a report.

An interesting sidebar is the fact that the FBI supplies information to some credit agencies and bureaus in the area of hundreds of thousands of requests per day. In return, said agencies supply the FBI with fingerprints and information they have obtained in their thorough techniques. At one time or another, laws have been proposed to make it illegal for this swap of information between the FBI and private agencies but most of these laws have fallen by the wayside.

When you apply for a loan or many jobs you sign a waiver allowing the institution or the prospective employer to employ such investigative or credit reports or verify any of your statements. Normally they will do so if you sign such a waiver. If the job requires any bonding, they definitely will check.

Many low paying jobs or even middle management jobs do not go to this extent, but in America large corporations often do go to the expense and bother of compiling such a report to screen out potential troublemakers before they become entrenched at the company. Some major corporations employ these reports when an employee is being considered for a raise or an important promotion.

In the early days of credit reporting, these reports were compiled and added to a consumer's file with no notification to the consumer himself. Since the FCRA it is now a law that if any subscriber or client requests an investigative report on a consumer, the agency must notify the consumer of this request.

If you receive such a notification, immediately submit a written request by certified mail to the agency or bureau and ask for a full description of the investigation including what kind of questions will be asked and to whom they will be asked. They must respond within five days of receipt of your letter.

Once you get this response you have the right to object to types or particular questions that will be asked. The normal procedure in this case is to try and convince the company that the type of information they are seeking has little or no effect on the loan application, promotion, job or whatever it is you are applying for. They may compromise and modify the investigation somewhat in regard to your request.

You do have the right to stop the investigation and not have this information entered in the file. Of course the loan or promotion will then fall through.

If an investigative report is preformed on you, you have the right to know what it says, with a couple of exceptions. These exceptions include when an insurance agency compiles a report using its own investigators. They do not have to show you anything at all. There are a couple other minor classifications that fall in the exception category.

If the report that is compiled on you is negative, and results in disqualification or can be said to be injurious (this is the key word) to your credit file, you must be allowed to view the contents of the file, free of charge. This is similar as to what happens when a non-investigative negative report is furnished.

They do not have to tell you the names of the people who were interviewed for the report nor do they have to divulge medical information they have compiled about you.

The law also does not state you can necessarily get a copy of the file, just that you are allowed to view it. Some agencies will not mail a file to you but will require you to come in person to view the file.

Non-investigative credit reports - those that compose the bulk of credit information in this country - are compiled with information from groups known as automatic subscribers. This means every time they come into contact with the consumer in any context regarding credit or opening a bank account, they automatically turn this information over to the credit bureau or agency. These automatic subscribers include most large banks, large department stores, finance loan companies, companies that refinance your house, collection agents, savings and loan institutions and some travel and entertainment cards (T & E cards).

These are the normal sources for credit reports but are not limited entirely to these institutions. Many credit bureaus also include judgments against you, liens against your house, probation or parole arrangements, wage garnishments, anything that is public information and available at the courthouse or through the county clerk.

If you have any interest in discovering this type of information on your own or seeing what is available on you and your friends, I will take a moment to plug "How To Get Anything on Anybody" by Lee Lapin, which is also published by C.E.P.

Now that we see where credit information comes from, must we assume that every time you have contact with any financial institution, such information is forwarded to a credit bureau? No, not necessarily. There are a number of institutions that simply do not report to credit bureaus. These include major oil companies and American Express. Many insurance companies do not deal with credit bureaus because they like to keep their information proprietary and inhouse. Rent payments are not normally reported. Medical bills, unless you miss payments and they are then turned over for collection are not reported. Savings or checking account information cannot be gotten from a credit report nor do small banks or utility companies generally report to credit bureaus.

If you default on payment to any of these organizations and they go to a third party or even an inhouse collection agency, they will definitely report it to all credit agencies within their reach.

Banks do not run credit reports on customers' checking or savings accounts, but they will run a report on any application for loans. Because of the expense banks often will not rerun or re-pull credit reports for additional loans, assuming you have a good record with them on any monies they have lent to you up to this point.

CREDIT REPORT FORMATS

When a subscriber, be it an employer or a lending institution, receives a credit report from their particular credit agency, they expect it to consist of a number of points. All credit agencies and bureaus have these points or some slight variation of them in common. When reading or examining the credit report, it is important to know what to expect and what should be on the report.

The first section normally is composed of the information used to identify you, the subject of the report. This section will consist of your complete name, your current address or the address you used in the application, previous address if there is one (especially if you've been less than two years at your present one), your social security number and date of birth.

The reason for this amount of identifying information is that errors do occur in birthdates, social security numbers or duplication of names, be they honest errors from a clerk, bad handwriting, a transition in numbers or deliberate errors by a consumer trying to hide credit history by transposing or changing numbers. Computers will compare the names and the numbers and if a match is made on a couple of the items, they will often assume it is you or will come back and ask you for your correct social security number and identification.

The next thing many credit reports contain is often overlooked but is a very important factor in credit history and this is the number of times subscribers have inquired about your credit history. These inquiries are regulated by states as to the amount of time they can span, the normal extent is 12 months.

These are important because it gives any subscriber a clear idea of your past credit activities and the number of times you have applied and/or the number of times you have been turned down for credit. If you have a number of denied applications, chances of the new one being denied increase logarithmically. If previous applications have been denied and the new credit score is quite high, a good credit manager will question the new score. Has the applicant wised up? Is he lying about something? Why were the other applications denied or has something changed to the extent that they might now consider giving you credit?

Following this will be a history of any collection attempts, liens, bankruptcies or other public records that have been issued against you.

Next will be a section consisting of your credit history. This history consists of such items as the names, dates any credit accounts were opened, the credit limits of these accounts, the terms originally issued as well as the balance outstanding, your monthly payment schedule and how you have preformed on that schedule. These performances are rated as to promptness (one, two or three month late indications). Any other irregularities will also be found in this section.

The history section will consider items pertaining to if your accounts were joint or individual, who else claimed responsibility for the account, if a co-signer was required because the original institution did not want to approve your credit for the limit, if you had any criminal convictions or even records of arrest or indictment (these are valid for seven years after the event is resolved meaning after parole, probation or sentence is finished). Any disputes you have entered on charges will be listed.

If you have refused or simply not paid an account and the lender has written it off, this will be recorded. If you have pledged anything as security on a loan this will be included along with the account or packet number. This is the number assigned to you for any particular loan.

The final section in a credit report is one not often found and one about which most people are not even aware, but can be included on a credit report. This final section is known as the "consumer statement."

You, as a consumer, have a right by law to include any statement up to 100 words in length about anything you wish to clarify on your credit report. You get to include your side of any dispute. This is an important part of any attempted repair work.

PHYSICAL REPAIR

There are a number of things one can do to improve or completely clean up their credit rating. We'll list them in this section and include the methods used by credit consultants, the so-called credit clearing agencies, many attorneys, as well as some of the less reputable approaches used by some people.

If you have applied for credit in any form and a credit report has been run on your request and credit is subsequently denied, you have the legal right to examine your credit report within 30 days of the denial for inaccuracies or reasons for which to reply.

Each and every time a person applies for a loan or credit and it is rejected, the institution that rejected it must provide written notice of the rejection along with on what inclination the credit bureau used to base this rejection.

If this happens to you, take the written notice of denial, photocopy it and send it in with a written request for a copy of your credit file. Note our sample written request page.

In dealing with credit bureaus it is a good idea to mail everything certified and keep a copy of all correspondence.

The law states that a credit bureau must inform you of what is contained in your credit report upon request. It does not state that they have to show you the actual report. Most bureaus will provide you with a copy of the report by mail once they process the request. If this copy does not appear in two weeks, either call or mail a follow-up letter asking for the original request to be filled.

An alternate method is not to request a copy of your report by mail but call and set up an appointment with the credit bureau, specifically for the purpose of you and your credit report. Most credit bureaus will do this with no hassle and will cooperate in both showing the report and subsequent action which may straighten out any discrepancies. It is wise to make an appointment rather than just stroll in and request the report. This service is free as long as you can prove with your photocopy you have been denied credit within the last 30 days due to a report by that credit bureau.

What happens if you haven't been denied credit within the last 30 days? You can still see your credit report from any and all credit bureaus by paying a modest fee, normally $10.00.

In order to view your credit report, you must establish what credit bureaus are active in your area. A simple way is to open the yellow pages and look them up. You will usually find a field office of one of the listed major bureaus in operation. This is a good place to start. If there are numerous working credit bureaus, you can inquire from your bank or any institution on which you plan to make a credit demand, what bureau or bureaus they use. Most will give you this information and this establishes a starting point to actually check your credit rating.

Once you've decided which bureaus to approach, follow the format we've detailed for contacting the bureau and requesting the copy. In this case, you should call them first and inquire what their charges are for reviewing a credit report. Enclose a check or money order with your request or alternately make an appointment and plan to pay the fee in person.

Once a copy of the report is obtained, read it over. If you've gone to the bureau in person you have the advantage of being able to ask the clerk who has furnished you with the copy, what abbreviations and inhouse designations stand for. Different bureaus use their own system of computer abbreviation. There is no universal format and as such it is sometimes difficult to decipher what each abbreviation stands for. Be sure to question any entry you don't understand or any numbers that don't correlate to what you think they should.

Once you have established what the report says about you, a good thing to do is check the credit inquiry section. It is possible for people to run credit reports on you without your authorization. This is illegal but, nevertheless, some organizations such as used car dealers and other not totally reputable concerns that are seeking information on a possible sales prospect, do this.

If there are credit inquiries that you did not authorize by signing an authorization form, you should ask the credit bureau of the name and address of the person and company who made the inquiries. Any unauthorized entry may be disputed by contacting the subscriber who asked for the run and advising them they are in violation of the Fair Reporting Credit Act and have made illegal inquiries into your credit history. Advise them to remove such entries immediately. Normally they will do this as prosecution may follow such a request.

The credit bureau itself may assist in removing illegal credit entries and/or may chastise subscribers if they feel their services are being misused.

If the credit inquiry section seems to be kosher and the pertinent facts about your personal history such as name, social security number, etc. are correct, move on to the payment history section and see if it contains any negative information about your ability and past record in regards to paying debts. If there is negative history and it is true, all is not lost. There are a number of methods involved to remove such information from your file.

The first thing to look at is the time involved in negative information. By law derogatory or bad information must be automatically removed from your credit file after a certain period of time has elapsed. This law is designed to let people under the capitalistic system recover from bankruptcy, liens, bad decisions or bad marriages, once they have proved themselves to be valuable members of society. Most credit bureaus remove this information automatically by computer when the dates have passed.

The law states that bankruptcies may remain on your credit history for ten years from the date of bankruptcy. A sidebar here is that bankruptcies do not necessarily cancel your ability to get credit. Some institutions actually prefer to see a bankruptcy on a credit report for the simple reason that you cannot file bankruptcy again for seven years so they know they have a very good chance of collecting any outstanding debts by threatening severe legal action, knowing you cannot resort to the bankruptcy courts a second time.

In general, these types of institutions that offer credit to bankruptcy victims are selling high priced or heavy markup items and as such are willing to grant the credit often with the idea of allowing you to establish positive credit by paying them off, which if they report to a credit bureau will actually do to some extent. It's a wise idea to examine any deal offered to people who have used the bankruptcy system closely to make sure that you are not over paying for the items involved. Most major credit card companies will not issue credit to someone who has file bankruptcy.

Other negative items which could include judgments or late payments in your credit history, repossessions and/or legal convictions, must be removed after seven years from the date of the occurrence or from the ending of parole or probation. If you have something of this nature on your credit history, check the dates and make sure they have compiled with this section of the Fair Credit Reporting Act.

Now after telling you the good news, there's also an exception that most consumers are not aware of. The exception is that any credit bureau may give away your entire credit history including those points of negative information that preclude the ten and seven year reporting limits respectively if a subscriber can prove he is questioning your application with regards to any credit transaction, including lines of credit or loans from a bank that involved $50,000 or more or in the case of life insurance, if the policy itself exceeds the $50,000 limit. The worst exception is if you are applying for a job of any sort with an annual salary of $20,000 or more, the credit bureau may legally report all negative history regardless of the time limits involved.

HOME OFFICE ADDRESSES FOR THE TOP 5 CREDIT BUREAUS

1. TRW Credit Information Services
   505 City Parkway West
   Orange, CA 92667
   (714) 991-5100

2. CBI/EQUIFAX
   P. O. Box 4091
   Atlanta, Georgia 30302
   (404) 329-1725

3. Trans Union Credit Information
   444 No. Michigan Avenue
   Chicago, Illinois 60611

4. Chelton Creditmatic Systems
   12606 Greenvile Avenue
   Dallas, Texas

5. Associated Credit Services Inc.
   652 E. North Belt Suite 400
   Houston, Texas 77060
   (715) 878-1900

COUNTER BALANCING THE RATIO

It is possible to add things to your credit report that are true or at least that an institution will verify by asking they be added. The law is vague on whether credit bureaus have to add items by request or not. The FTC has held a number of findings requiring credit bureaus to add positive reports wherein they may counterbalance unfavorable reports that resulted in injury to your credit rating.

Some credit bureaus will charge a slight fee for adding these favorable items but it is certainly worth a few dollars in order to help repair the credit picture.

In order to do this, you must personally contact any creditors with whom you have had a good repayment relationship, and ask them to list this information on your credit report. Once they have agreed verbally to do this, you contact the credit bureau and inform them of the availability of this information and ask they contact the institution or creditor directly to verify it. Obviously they won't just take your word for it but they will attempt to verify this information and add it to your report.

It is possible to update employment history in this same manner. If you have added outside income, taken another job, added a part time job, or are making money doing freelance work and can prove it or have an employer who will verify it, it is possible to get the credit bureau to add this information to your credit history.

These steps should produce a much better if not totally clean credit report that you can use as a basis to build further credit history. Once you have established a favorable credit report you can contact the credit bureau involved and ask them to send a copy of your new and improved report to anyone who has initiated a credit check on you within the last six months. In the case of employers, they will do this over the last two years.

This is true even if you are not currently requesting credit from this institution and is a good idea to both update your reputation as well as keep an accurate report in the hands of people with whom you may wish to further conduct business.

This is an accurate summation of the aboveboard methods to clean up a person's credit and will work in 90% of all cases. Note these methods may be used on your own credit history, or for a fee, can be used to upgrade the reports of another.

Once you understand the theory and techniques involved in credit upgrade, it's a good idea to check your own report every eight or nine months to make sure it is remaining accurate and is upgraded as is expected.

THE TRICK

Credit counseling agencies or credit cleaning agencies or consultants who advise they will improve your credit for a set fee, (one should note these fees often run several hundred dollars) operate on a simple premise; any and all negative history on a consumer's credit file must be investigated and resubstantiated at any time the consumer requests the agency to do so. This means, if you compose a letter (see our sample) claiming you disagree with certain items on your credit history and these items are "injurious to your credit rating" and mail this complaint by certified mail to your credit bureau, they have a "reasonable" period of time to investigate all disputes the consumer originates.

This time period is usually construed as four to six weeks. They are required to contact individually each subscriber and ask for a re-verification of the charge. Why is this to your advantage? Because many subscribers do not feel it is worth their time to respond to the high number of inquiries from people doing just this thing and will simply not answer the letter in the required time period, especially if they have already written off the debt.

Most institutions keep financial records for about two years. If you are disputing a late payment or a charge off that happened after they have already thrown away their records on the transaction, there is no way they can prove the fact this transaction is still bad. You might have paid it off since their records were destroyed and they have no record of that, in which case they will not respond to the letter.

Institutions, especially banks, have a limited number of people working in the credit department. Their time is budgeted on a priority basis and when they are too busy, they will not bother to answer these letters knowing it is something no one will complain about in the future. Occasionally clerks make errors and do not answer the letters or cannot find the files.

Some, so-called credit counselors, will concentrate on the month of December or August in which to request a large number of subscriber verifications knowing that in December many credit managers are taking the holidays off and in August they may be further weakened by vacations in the department.

How does this benefit you, the consumer? On an average basis 50% of all negative information will be removed from your credit file following the first verification inquiry letter. This means if you go to a counselor or so-called professional and pay a fee, four to six weeks later he can show you a new credit report that will contain an average of 50% fewer negative items. This may be enough to immediately transpose you from a negative credit risk to a positive credit risk to many institutions.

If this first inquiry still does not provide the consumer with a clear enough record, the counselor will wait a few weeks and resubmit a verification letter on the remaining items. There is no legal limit as to how many times this can be done and each time the credit bureau must contact the subscribers and the subscribers must answer within the reasonable amount of time allowed. The first time the subscriber fails to answer the letter within the reasonable amount of time, the negative item is removed from your credit report permanently.

Using this simple technique of diligence and follow through, it is often possible to completely clear your credit report in a manner of weeks or months.

There is no legal restriction on the personnel involved in such transactions. You, as a consumer, may preform the action equally as efficiently as any credit counselor or attorney without paying the fees.

Why doesn't this happen more often? Simply because most consumers have no knowledge of the Fair Credit Reporting Act or not enough knowledge to come up with this system. This is normally the only type of effort utilized by people who advertise as credit counselors or credit consultants.

OTHER HONORABLE SOLUTIONS

After blitzing the credit bureaus with a number of verification requests, if there are still persistent negative subscribers listed on the credit report, request the names, addresses and phone numbers of each subscriber who is supplying negative history.

At this point it is possible and often advisable for the consumer to contact a subscriber in person. This should be arranged over the phone explaining there is a problem and politely requesting an appointment with someone who has the ability to negotiate these items. This is usually a credit manager or someone in an equally prominent position.

Remember the subscriber himself has the legal opportunity to cancel any negative information he has provided, with or without the assistance of the credit bureau.

If you have a late payment or a series of late payments to a scriber and you have since paid them off and have continued a mutually agreeable relationship with the subscriber, the effort involved in contacting them personally will often impress the credit manager enough that he will agree to remove the negative history because you have now proven yourself a reliable consumer. They may want to keep your business.

You can point out the fact that the manager does not necessarily take his time to write a letter to the bureau asking to remove negative input, but he can simply choose to not respond to the upcoming inquiry from the bureau that you will initiate.

Another approach is to offer the subscriber payment in full for any debt or balance remaining on your transaction if he will in turn remove the entire transaction from the credit bureau's report.

The key phrase here is to be sure the manager understands and agrees to remove the transaction from the report or not respond to an inquiry rather than showing the problem has been paid in one lump sum. If he does the latter this payment record will still remain on your credit report and will irritate the credit bureau along with other potential creditors when they easily figure out the method you have taken in order to achieve this end. It is legally viable and ethical to ask them to remove the transaction in return for a payment for the outstanding debt.

In some instances the subscriber may refuse to do so because he has signed an agreement with the credit bureau to the effect that this sort of action will not be taken. This is generally a dead end and unless you can convince the credit manager it is in his best interest to not respond or remove the transaction, there is no legal way to pursue this.

At this point, if you are unable or unwilling to resolve the outstanding negative items, write a brief (under 100 words) erudite statement and ask for it to be included in your credit report. A credit bureau by law must include such a statement. It should be pointed out that even the best written statement does not necessarily cancel the effects of unpaid bills, but in a legitimate disputed area, can convince the new potential creditor there was some grounds for the problem and he is unlikely to encounter this with you.

BANKRUPTCIES

Any publicly reported debt, bankruptcies, judgments, etc., is subject to not only the inaccuracies of the credit bureau who picks up the report but the inaccuracies that the government or bureaucracy who initiated and recorded the report. Be certain to check all such judgments very carefully with your own files to discover if they are correct. Many credit counselors deny all bankruptcies, liens or judgments with the same fervor they have questioned the credit history negative aspects. In many cases they are correct and there are inaccuracies in the bankruptcy which must be corrected by the same methods just detailed. The subscriber must verify judgments, liens, or bankruptcies or the item will be removed from the consumer's credit file.

There is one loophole in the Fair Credit Reporting Act with regards to updating files. Credit bureaus may ignore any request they feel are irrelevant or frivolous. The Federal Government has taken a dim view of turn downs for this reason and will investigate to see if they really are frivolous or irrelevant.

If the credit bureau suspects the series of letters inquiring about the consumer's history are initiated by a credit counselor or a credit attorney, they will sometimes reply this constitutes harassment or other legal terms and they will refuse to follow through on this reporting. If this happens, it is wise to file a calm follow-up letter that states this has been injurious to your credit history and is in no way irrelevant or frivolous and you request the subscriber be contacted and this bad debt be verified.

If they still refuse to do this, the next step is to contact the Federal Trade Commission (we have included the addresses of local Federal Trade Commissions) with a copy of your request and their responses. The FTC does have a regulatory function with regard to credit bureaus and will follow-up on any complaints initiated by consumers. Most credit bureaus would rather do their job and make subscribers verify debts, especially if there is any risk of inaccuracy, than risk the ire of the FTC.

CREDIT SCORING; BRASS TACKS

Because each institution that issues loans or credit or independent scoring agencies use their own validation system and because each system is subject to change every three or four years, this list is by no means a positive requirement list but rather a general overview that will allow you to give yourself an arbitrary credit score. It will be within the ballpark of most credit scoring agencies.

Most credit card issuing institutions will want to see a disposable income each month of about half of your take home income before issuing cards. Judge yourself on the following list. You should score at least 17 points to be above the gray area in most credit card scoring systems.

	Pts
Telephone listed in your name.	2
Married.	2
Dependents, none	0
1 - 3.	2
4 or more.	1
Age Group	
21 - 25.	1
40 - 64.	2
over 65.	1
Years at present residence	
to 5 years.	1
over 5 years.	2

Years at previous address

less than 5 years 1

more than 5 years 2

Years at present job

less than 1 year 1

1 - 3 years 2

4 - 6 years 3

7 - 10 years 4

over 10 years 5

Spouse employed 2

Monthly obligations (incl. rent or mortgage)

less than $500 2

over $500 1

Type of work

Professions, executive 4

Skilled worker 3

Blue collar 2

All others 1

Loan Experience

At bank where you apply for credit 5

At another bank 3

Checking or savings account at bank you want credit 2

It is possible to determine from the above chart how to enhance your overall credit picture for scoring purposes as well as what areas can be solidified to establish the fact you are a good risk.

Occupation can be a major factor in determining credit. Beside the years on the job, the type of job itself is quite important. There are no solid rules here either as a loan officer or clerk in an issuing institution will have an arbitrary list of occupations they like to see and occupations they don't like to see. Some generalities can be extracted by reading several of these lists: the best occupations as far as many institutions are concerned are doctors, accountants, engineers, CEO's or top level management, office and factory supervisors, teachers, nurses, pharmacists, civil service workers, sometimes military as military people can be forced to pay under threat of court martial, trained and skilled workers, dentists, followed by policemen, firemen, factory supervisors or skilled machinists and media personnel and electricians.

Categories they do not like to see include the following: actors, bartenders, self-employed people, unskilled factory workers, cooks, gas station attendants, beauticians, waitresses, taxi drivers, hospital orderlies, nurse's assistants, practical nurses, porters, musicians, laborers, house painters, amusement park employees, hotel employees except for upper eschelon management, minors, retirees, anything with the word free lance in front of it or students. If there is a more creative way to list your job classification so it appears to fall into one of the upper categories, by all means consider doing so.

Occasionally people will ask their boss or personnel officer of the company they work for to do them a favor and verify their employment at a higher rate. This is also true on the length of their employment. If you have a good relationship with the person in charge, this costs them nothing and will often enhance your feelings towards the company and your impetus to do a good job.

Additionally, part-time income is counted on credit card scoring sheets and should be included if your disposable income ratio is not at the correct level. Part-time income can include: carpentry, painting, free lance writing, free lance photography, any occupation that is difficult to verify and seems applicable to your present status. Spouses can have part-time or free lance work if they do not have a verifiable job.

Some companies may ask for automobile data. This will include the age of the automobile. The newer the model the higher points one scores. This is unfair if you drive a collector's Corvette or something similar that is worth more than a new Corvette. You will not get any points for it.

Negative items on your credit history will subtract points. More than two or three credit inquiries without subsequent credit being granted within the last year will subtract points. Finance company loans will give you negative points and the more loans you have, the more negative points will be accumulated.

On rare occasions systems will grant more points if you have more than one telephone at your residence or listed in your name.

CREDIT APPLICATION NO NO'S

TURN-OFFS TO ANY LOAN OFFICER

>Minors

>Alcoholics

>People with a Drug Conviction

>Lots of Address Changes

>Lots of Employment Changes

>P. O. Boxes for Addresses

>Persons with Only a Medium or Less Level Income with Too Many Charge Cards (even if there is no balance) on the cards

>People Working at Brand New Businesses or which have not been established long

>Enlisted Military Personnel who are not officers or at least NCO's

>High Debt Income Averages

>Bankruptcies

>Chapter 13 Filings

>Non-citizens

>People who Work at Unskilled Jobs

People whose Business Address Is the Same as their Residence, even though they say they are not self-employed

Mail Drops or Residence Hotels for Home Addresses (if the loan officer is sharp enough to pick this out)

SECONDARY CREDIT REPORTS

There is a phenomena in the credit reporting business known as a secondary (or computer generated) credit report. Occurring naturally, these reports are the product of an over abundance of credit information and the peculiarities of computer retrieval systems.

Due to the large number of people in the United States and the large number of credit reports generated by constant credit reporting and upgrading, computers used by credit bureaus do not search through files to find a complete name, social security number and address.

Rather different credit agencies use different formats all based on a code or file number for each individual consumer.

This code normally consists of the first initial or two of one's last name, the same with the first name, possibly the middle initial, the first couple of numbers of the current address, a couple initials of one's street, town, state, and one to three numbers of one's social security number. This information is all run together to produce approximately twenty or so combined alphabetical/numerical codes. This code may seem non-sensical at first glance but actually contains all relevant information needed to identify each individual consumer regardless of the duplication of names.

Each time a subscriber requests a credit check from any particular credit bureau, the computer is given the file code or name and then searches its banks for a match. Because the code begins with the consumer's last name and then progresses through the address, the computer will pull anything close to this code as well as exact matches. It will not normally pull alternate choices but simply state no record exists if a certain number of digits do not match with the request.

THE L. A. LAW TRICK

A few years ago a couple of now famous industry attorneys in Los Angeles discovered holes inherent in this system of file retrieval making it possible that no file may be found for a particular person and thusly a new file will automatically be created by the credit bureau. In this manner one person may have many files existing simultaneously each with different credit information contained on each.

When the attorneys discovered there were far more files on file than there are consumers in America, they grasped the weakness in this system and began exploiting it.

After researching the laws it was determined the existence of more than one credit report (or secondary reports) whether created intentionally or computer generated, does not constitute an illegal act.

This would not be true if the secondary file was used to commit fraud. The simple existence or creation of a secondary file, assuming that factual information only is used, does not constitute fraud nor appear to break any laws.

In order to capitalize on this idea, the attorneys decided when presented with a credit file that seemed to be beyond the avenues of normal upgrading (which we've already detailed), instead of waiting the time required for negative information to be legally dropped or paying the debts off and negotiating the cancelling of debit information, it would be possible to create a secondary file, slipping through the law.

They began charging fees, sometimes $3,000 or $4,000, to create secondary files for their customers, or rather to advise their customers on the creation of such files.

They discovered the primary variables involved in computer retrieval of a consumer's file, are either the address and the zip code run together in one file or the name and social security number run together as one file. In order to create secondary files they advised their clients to either create a new address for themselves by using a relative's or friend's address or by simply renting a mail drop in a nearby town.

Such drops are now available universally and do provide legitimate addresses for receiving mail and in some cases could be construed as a legal residence.

Once a new address is procured, or once several new addresses are procured, the applicant could then go to a credit bureau and request a copy of his file, using his correct name but listing the new address as his new address and another alternate address as his previous residence.

If the check comes back as no report available, no record on file, he then would carefully make note of the exact information supplied the bureau to get that report. Then go out and start a new credit history.

Another method that saves dealing with the credit bureau itself, thereby possibly incurring suspicion from a clerk who notices too many inquiries in one name, is simply to go out and apply for minor credit cards or store credit cards or try and buy a car at a number of car dealers until one comes back "no record."

Chances are they may not sell one a car at this point, but one then knows what name and address to employ to get a blank credit sheet. One begins to build credit on this sheet and in a couple of months one should be able to supply several concrete, truthful credit references without falsifying any records or changing one's name or social security number.

In some instances, people do change their surname, their middle name, their middle initials, drop a middle name, or transpose the first digits of their social security number.

If it could be proven this was done deliberately in order to commit fraud, it would be illegal. However, a simple transposition of a social security number from memory is certainly not prosecuted nor does it even appear suspicious. This has the same effect as changing addresses.

Most legitimate credit counselors do not advise this sort of credit tampering to develop a secondary file. It does, however, appear to be legal, and may or may not be morally justified. One only needs to suffer through a series of negative responses or life changing decisions due to false or inaccurate credit reports to have one's moral standards suffer through a fast period of readjustment.

Once the secondary file is in use, it becomes the primary file and that information is regurgitated everytime a credit report is required. The old file remains buried on a disk somewhere until automatic flags trip the updating process and the computer wipes out the credit history.

In this way a secondary file completely replaces the original file and becomes one's primary source of credit history.

Variations on the above theme occur when a person, normally a woman, gets married and changes her name legally, thereby beginning a new credit report. She simply omits the information on her maiden name and/or previous addresses or changes the information to fit the new file.

It's also possible to legally change your name. There has been much published on the ability of Americans to change their name by assuming a new name or filing a registered pen name paper with the court.

Most credit applications do not ask if you've had credit under another name or previous names. Generally speaking you are then not committing fraud by legally adopting a new name and beginning a new credit history with that name.

A QUICK TRICK - SIXTY DAY CREDIT

It is possible to develop several solid credit references and give yourself a good, albeit quick credit history by following an unusual plan. This advice is often given by some of the shadier attorneys and you could expect to pay several hundred dollars for this advice.

Allow at least 60 days to put this plan into motion and you'll need about $1,000 cash to make the plan work. You do get the cash back. It does not go anywhere. It is a short-term investment to help establish your credit references.

Approach an office of a major banking chain and open a savings account in your name using your correct information or at least the information you want to appear on your new credit history with your $1,000. (It is possible to do this with less money but $1,000 tends to fall in the category where you will receive a high rating from the credit reporting agency as they don't list the exact amount. They use codes to indicate how much money is in the account and $1,000 is a substantial savings account although it is possible to use less in some instances.)

After you've opened the account wait a week for the paperwork to go through and approach a loan officer of the bank where you now have a savings account. Explain to the officer you have a number of loans or out-standing debts you wish to pay off since they are charging higher rates than you are making in the savings account. You'd like to pledge your savings account for a loan to pay off these debts.

It is common practice to allow 100% security on loans within the same institution where a savings account is held as security. The bank should grant you a loan for the full

$1,000 at the current rate for secured loans. This will be two to three times more than the interest the savings account is paying but you have your $1,000 back.

If you request a twelve-month loan, the loan payments are reasonable and there is little paperwork involved. The net difference you are paying is only a few percent from the savings account to the loan.

Most banks will not run a credit check on the applicant at this point since the loan is 100% secured within house funds. Be sure to list the information you want on your credit history, especially if you are creating an alternate file or any of the other options used by persons rebuilding their credit.

After you've received your loan, go to another bank similar to the first one, re-deposit, wait a week and take a loan on the same terms from this new bank. Of course, you do not mention your previous loan at their competition.

Once this has happened, wait a little while and then go to a third bank and repeat the procedure. Wait a week or two and make your loan at this third bank. Now take your floating $1,000 and open a checking account at one of the three banks where you have a loan, preferably one that issues Visa or MasterCards, if this is one of your goals.

A week later make a payment on each of your loans from the checking account. A week after that make another payment and a week later make your third payment. These are actually costing you nothing since they will be subtracted from the outstanding balance on your loan, loans having minimum or 0 pre-payment penalty.

After the third week you will have established a paying pattern and will have established a credit report. Your credit at each of these banks will now be excellent because you have actually pre-paid three payments in the space they did not even require a first payment. This will give you almost four months of pre-payment and any potential issuing institution will view the fact you pay well in advance (the first payment won't be due until a month or two after you open the loan) with favor.

It is now possible to begin obtaining credit cards on your newly created excellent credit history. It makes sense to apply for the easiest cards first, these being oil company, local retail cards and then cards from larger retail chains. Once you have gotten a number of these, you can apply for Visa or Mastercharge and generally you will find these will carry you through as the banks prefer to do an infile report, checking on the creditors you listed, if there are enough of them which in this case there are, rather than running a credit history report which will cost them money.

When applying for your credit cards, both regional and national in scope, stagger your applications. Don't send in more than one application every few days and be certain to list all your savings accounts on the credit application so they will not pull a credit report but just use the information you have provided to establish credit.

This is a "quick fix" and will not work for large unsecured lines of credit or large unsecured bank loans, but will establish credit so you can get credit cards to allow you to build credit history from there.

SKIN SHEDDING

This information is given for the purposes of information only and we do not advise anyone to use these procedures without checking with a lawyer first.

The simplest method of skin shedding is to create a new identity. There are a number of good books written on this field. Specifically those published by Eden Press in Fountain Valley, California and Loomponics in Washington are excellent sources of materials on identity.

It is possible to concoct and procure a new identity in almost any name one wishes, change social security numbers and addresses to build a new credit report.

The second system some people take advantage of is to contact credit bureaus where they have a negative credit report and then advise them they have misinformation listed in the section where they identify the consumer. After the credit bureau changes its policy to reflect what the consumer has said is his correct social security number or name, he allows some time to elapse and then contacts the credit bureau to claim they have false information on his report. In fact, none of that information belongs to him but must be attributed to someone else with the same name.

At this point the credit bureau will contact the subscribers as we've detailed previously to verify information, discover the information does not correlate and drop the file. A few months later the person generally contacts the credit bureau again and has them re-correct his information per the original entry, which by this time contains a clear credit history since the subscribers did not verify and the items have been dropped.

SEMINARS: TALKING FOR MONEY

In addition to the lucrative field of credit counseling or direct credit repair services, there is an additional opportunity for making a substantial income in this field. As advised by numerous organizations that purport to teach credit counseling, it is possible to arrange to give seminars to people who wish to learn about credit, repair their own credit, or become credit counselors themselves.

An important fact to note here is there is no regulation whatsoever on giving seminars as you are not actually involved with repairing anyone's credit. You are simply passing on the necessary information for a consumer to do it.

Obviously the information you would be passing on would be exactly what is included in this book although some sections should probably remain, ah, personal.

In order to make money in this fashion you lay out a lesson plan, spend some time talking on your own, tape a speech, give your proposed seminar in front of a group of friends at least once and encourage them to ask any and all questions which come to mind to make sure you have a grasp of the field and can answer their questions. We do not advise anyone giving false information or going into this business unless you are confident you actually can help someone.

The numbers involved can be staggering: the average price for credit repair is about $400; the average price for a credit seminar is between $300 and $500.

The seminars contain no proprietory or secret information. They simply show the various means of manipulating your credit file under the Fair Credit Reporting Act and in addition provide lists of secured credit cards, banks looking to issue credit cards, and answer questions from consumers on the credit industry.

The normal route is to join one of the so-called credit counseling groups that will "give" you a book for $100 (up) explaining the Fair Credit Reporting Act and pass along some information on planning a seminar and placing your ads.

Seminars normally take more than one session. There is an introductory seminar for which a small fee is charged and is designed to encourage customers to pay the additional fee and attend the other seminars.

This course can take an one 8-hour day or can be spread over two or three evenings. Often the latter approach is better as people retain more knowledge and feel they are getting more for their money if they come to a place more than once. This is balanced off in expenses by the cost of renting a meeting room and providing the necessary services.

If you join one of the consumer counseling groups, you'll get their book, their lesson plans, sometimes contracts, sample letters, for a rather substantial fee. They encourage you to place ads in newspapers (normally display ads) offering your introductory seminar on credit.

These agencies predict you can draw 15 - 20 people into a seminar program. If you are charging $500 per person (minus whatever you are paying the "backing" group for the privilege of using their lesson books and/or quizzes and the cost of the room itself) the remainder is profit.

The problem with this idea is that it's been done for awhile now and attendance may be falling off in your area. Newspaper ads cost money and you'll soon discover if you have to place one additional display ad, it cuts into your profit margin severely. Once you have rented a meeting room for $100 - $400 depending on the city (usually in a hotel) you are committed to try to make back the expenses of the ad and the room. If only one or two people show up you still have to give the seminar you have contracted to give unless you put in a disclaimer stating you won't unless a specified number of people show up, in either case you will lose money. Perhaps as much as $1,000 to $2,000 that you've spent in preparation fees.

If 10 - 25 people do show up, you can see from the numbers that the profit potential is enormous. Oddly enough, most people will feel they have spent their $400 - $500 wisely when they leave the seminar as long as you can talk in front of people and project the ideas covered in this book effectively.

In order for people to find out this information on their own, it would require a large investment in time and energy. They might never come up with the whole picture. It's worth it to many people to upgrade their credit and they will pay the seminar fees.

Many credit counselors and credit leaders have since switched to using classified ads, especially in the cheaper throw-away newspapers or local small papers in order to receive a wider exposure as they can run a number of classifieds for the price of one display. They can also get an idea of their attendance prior to actually renting the room.

There is another method most of these companies don't cover. If you are serious about giving seminars and making money, contact all the colleges in your area, especially any junior colleges, and ask if they have a continuing adult education department. Most colleges do.

These departments offer classes taught by professionals but not necessarily accredited teachers. Most of these class instructors have no specific qualifications for teaching. You don't have to be on the college staff. You simply have to have some knowledge in the field.

The system works thusly: you contact the college, give them a cover letter and a one page proposal, the name of your course or seminar, what you're going to teach and how much you are going to charge.

The average fee for these classes is $40 - $60. This includes from four to eight hours of instruction and most colleges will allow you to charge an additional fee for materials given or handed out at the meeting. The colleges themselves put your offering in their brochure which is mailed to hordes of potential students or residents in the area. The school will supply the classroom free of charge. Usually you split the gross income from the class with the school.

The good news is that you are not paying any advertising expenses, you are reaching a predetermined selection of potential students (often people who have attended classes before and know the setup) and you can repeat your class every semester.

This adult education format can draw anywhere from 10 - 60 students in a class. While the income may not be as high as it would be by doing your own seminar, the amount of risk is also considerably reduced. If six to ten different schools in your area list your class, you will find you are making anywhere from $300 to $1,000 a night, up to ten times a semester.

 Not a bad revenue for a part-time income.

To further expand this idea of co-sponsored seminars, you can contact any adult recreation departments around or you can contact clubs and organizations such as Kiwanis, and invite them to co-sponsor your seminar. If you can provide legitimacy for your claims, these organizations may include you in their mailings just as the colleges will, thereby becoming co-sponsors and allowing you to reap fairly good profits with zero risk.

Most of these organizations do publish a disclaimer to the effect they will cancel the class if a certain number of people do not register. It has been my experience that this rarely happens and any class of interest will not only draw but continue to draw for years providing a substantial income for motivated teachers.

Many organizations that suggest you give seminars, (credit counseling organizations) have fancy names for themselves, provide you with certificates upon graduation, may or may not give you a quiz or a test and then will certify you as a credit counselor. They will also provide initials that sound scholarly that can be added after your name.

If you feel it makes your appearance more legitimate, feel free to use my initials and become a certified credit specialist or CCS. If you want to become more creative, you could become a credit rehab administration benefactor, CRAB, or even a credit rehabilitation understudy demonstrator, CRUD.

You get the idea. . .

CREDIT UPDATE

TRW, the largest credit reporting agency in the world, has instituted an new, unusual program they call Credentials.

This program has some features never before offered to credit consumers in this country. For a mere pittance of $35 a year, TRW offers a package of services that includes unlimited access to one's credit file (or TRW's version of same) notification when anyone requests a credit check on you, protection from liability from stolen or lost cards and the "privilege" of taking part in a test all computer information network that will list such facts as the consumer's income, where they work, value of their assets including real and personal property, savings, etc.

In theory this network will give the consumer with good credit a positive resource to facilitate loans and lines of credit from issuers.

Several advantages to TRW are inherent in this arrangement. In the first place, the subscribers are paying $35 for a service they could access completely free of charge under federal law if they had been denied credit. Or, at worst case scenario, pay a $10 fee for a look at their current credit history. Many credit card holders do not realize their rights under this law and as such consider the $35 viewing fee a bargain.

The notification factor is also somewhat nullified by the law which requires the consumer's permission, except in certain unusual cases, for any credit search so notification becomes redundant.

Ditto with the insurance from theft and loss as again by law consumer's liability is limited to only $50 per card regardless of the prevailing circumstances.

In effect, TRW is marketing a service or more specifically a package of services they are required to provide anyway. A most interesting situation. Still, the most profitable aspect from TRW's standpoint at least, may be the new data base. This data base, unless subscribers specifically forbid it, will be sold to numerous mail order and retail merchants who wish to pinpoint an upscale market. Rental of this list allows the solicitors to pinpoint one's assets and enter into any potential marketing situation at an advantage. Early indications are this will be a very popular rental list and should generate not only junk mail but a number of sales proposals, ranging from high ticket items like stocks and bonds to the mail order gift catalogues that are currently popular.

A darker side to this new data base is the accepted loss of privacy and consolidation of personal and private information on a huge number of Americans.

Does the new data base actually facilitate the loan application process by providing a clearing house for needed credit history? Recently a consumer publication queried five of the largest companies, the names of which were provided by TRW as accepting loan information from this new data base. In each case all five companies said while they would look at the new information, they would require separate credit applications filled out and a separate credit check run on all applicants.

In other words, business as usual.

Will anyone subscribe to what appears on the surface to be a redundant and dubious program? As this is being written, 200,000 consumers in the state of California alone have paid their $35 fee and TRW expects 2,000,000 more to follow in their footsteps within the next couple years. Some social critics are suggesting this procedure is similar to ads which prey on lack of knowledge to sell unneeded services. Currently with this file TRW is expanding their subscriber marketing by claiming to have added nation-wide search capabilities. To quote a TRW ad, "Through a thorough, well planned process we have created an in-depth file that now has information on 138,000,000 credit active Americans from virtually every major population area.

Because of TRW's national on-going commitment to quality this data base is continually enlarged and updated." The ad fails to mention the other four major credit reporting agencies or the other 9,997 smaller credit reporting agencies that may not share the same information as does TRW.

OPTIMA: OPTIMIZING YOUR PLASTIC

In what can be viewed as a response to Visa and Mastercharge, introducing premium cards which compete directly with American Express and other Travel and Entertainment cards, American Express has introduced a mastercharge, sort of.

As rumored for years American Express has finally released a revolving charge card. Not only does this card compete directly with Visa and Mastercharge, it undercuts most bank credit cards by offering a lower interest rate on the unpaid balance.

Introduced at a low 13.5% interest, the Optima card will actually be geared to the prime rate. The interest will be adjusted semiannually and is to be kept at l.7 to 1.8 times the prime rate. This makes the Optima one of the cheapest, at least in terms of interest, bank cards in the country.

American Express can afford to keep the charge low because, at least at this point, they are only offering them to people who already hold a green, gold or platinum American Express card. By concentrating on their own customers whose payment history is on file, they minimize bad debts and losses to the new card.

The Optima is not cheap. True, the annual fee is only $15, however this must be added to the fact that you have to maintain one of the other levels of American Express card. At the moment annual fees are $45 for the green, $60 for the gold and $250 for the platinum. To be fair this fee must be considered along with the $15 Optima fee when judging it against bank credit cards.

American Express is keeping a low profile by insisting Optima will only be offered to holders of American Express cards and will not go into the marketplace and compete directly with Visa and Mastercharge. A number of Mastercharge and Visa spokespeople have indicated their skepticism to this plan and have gone on record as saying they see American Express as going into direct competition by changing the application criteria for the Optima card.

This card is a bonus to consumers if you are already paying a fee for an American Express card. It provides one of the lowest interest rates around for a reasonable $15 annual fee and it should be remembered that American Express does not subscribe to credit reporting agencies but keeps their own credit history so it is at least theoretically possible, if one falls into medium-to-high income bracket to obtain both these cards with a dubious MasterCard or Visa payment history.

A WORD TO THE WISE

In a most unusual move Visa and MasterCard have combined forces to institute a lawsuit against a California attorney who was allegedly advising his clients to take out as many bank cards as possible and enter fraudulent information on their application blanks. Reading between the lines, this sounds like the typical get-as-many-cards-as-you-can for the possibility of cashing out and generating a large lump sum and not naming the other cards on the application so it becomes obvious to the issuing institutions what is going on.

Enough said except the lawsuit is for $5,000,000.

Sears has joined the ranks of revolving bank type issuers instead of remaining a point-of-sale issuer as they have been. The Sears Financial Network has started issuing Discoverer cards. These cards are accepted in about three-quarters of a million stores all over the country, not just Sears stores but other department stores.

70 LITTLE KNOWN CREDIT FACTS

1. There is no such thing as a set credit rating. Each institution has a different method for calculating credit and will score each applicant differently than the competition. One can be turned down by credit at one place and accepted at another.

2. Unless you live in a community property state, no creditor may inquire about your martial status or about your spouse or spouse's earning power (unless you are claiming your spouse as part of your income) when you apply for an unsecured credit card or unsecured loan.

3. Unless there's a problem with one spouse refusing to pay or an account was opened based strictly on one spouse's income, a creditor cannot request a new application on a jointly held credit card or credit account simply because of a divorce or separation.

4. People applying for loans sometimes increase their paper value by legally establishing their own corporation. This can be done in the state of Delaware using a registered agent. Call the Delaware State Director of Corporations and ask for a list if you're interested. Or it can be done through an attorney in most states for under $1,000. The corporation then issues private stock and when applying for a loan the applicant lists a large ownership of this stock at a greatly inflated price. As there is no open trading on the stock most banks will take your word that the stock is issued by a legitimate corporation and is worth what the applicant claims it is worth.

5. On the average, Americans spend approximately 75% of their income each month repaying loans, debts and credit cards.

6. As this is being written, the United States government has phased out all currency in excess of $100 bills; $500, $1,000, $10,000 bills are rapidly becoming collector's items and soon will not be honored by monetary institutions.

7. It normally takes four to eight weeks to be issued either a secured or unsecured credit card after filing the application.

8. Up to 80% of all bankruptcies in this country are recorded with inaccurate facts at the courthouse.

9. When applying for credit or loans, age is a definite factor. The lowest scoring ages are under 25 and in one's 30's. The highest scoring times are past 40.

10. T & E cards such as American Express and Diner's Club rarely count for points in a credit application. Visa and Mastercharge always do.

11. If you list finance company loans or they appear in your credit history, they will give negative points on credit scoring even if you have faithfully repaid the loans. It is best to leave them off.

12. If you apply for a loan and you own your home, you should realize that credit reporting agencies do not differentiate between people who have heavy mortgages and people who have paid their home off entirely. Owning the home is a plus and is scored as such regardless of any out-standing mortgage.

13. You can add a favorable statement of 100 words to your credit report by paying a small fee to the credit reporting agency.

14. If credit cards are lost or stolen, the owner's liability is limited to $50 per card. If you have numerous cards it is a good idea to take out a credit card insurance policy for a nominal fee.

15. When applying for a credit card, if you take out an additional card for a spouse or a friend, you will be responsible for all payments on this card unless you take the card back and notify the institution in writing you are no longer responsible for the debts of your partner.

16. If you are being investigated for a job that you did not apply for - in other words, by a headhunting firm or someone simply checking on you to see if you fit a position, they do not have to notify you that an investigative or reporting credit history has been run.

17. Some institutions have separate scoring systems for persons under 30 in order to erase any built-in bias as people of this age normally do not have the same ownership or income as people over 40.

18. If you have an error in billing on a credit card report, do not write about it on a bill. Chances are it will not be noticed. Send a separate, preferably certified, letter to the issuing institution.

19. Some people stall by taking bills with magnetic, computerized identification numbers on them and rubbing this portion of the bill over a strong speaker magnet or electronic tape bulk demagnetizer. This will cause the computer to kick out the bill and delay the billing for a certain length of time until it can be rebilled.

20. In instances where there is no magnetic numbering system but rather an optical scan number, some people use an Exacto knife or razor blade to shave off part of the number. This will kick out the bill and delay the billing at no charge to the consumer.

21. If you have a credit purchase under $25,000 and the contract is sold to a third party such as a finance company or a bank, by law this third party is responsible for any written or implied warranties on the product. You can legally stop payment while this situation is being resolved just as if you were paying directly to the retailer or merchant rather than to a finance company.

22. It is possible to over-extend the credit limit on a credit card very easily by simply buying items under the floor limit of the card. This means they will not be called in and will not be deducted on the card until the end of the billing period. It is also possible to buy an item under the credit limit that is called in and then buy a number of items under the floor limit, usually $50 to $75, thereby running up the credit limit to two or three times its actual limitation on the card.

23. Forms to file your own bankruptcy can be purchased at any large stationery store and some bookstores.

24. If you are married and have separate debts in your own name, if you live in a community property state or move to a community property state, community property cannot be taken in payment of judgments against these separate debts. Community property states are: Arizona, California, Idaho, Louisiana, Montana, Nevada, New Mexico, Texas and Washington.

25. If you use a post-dated check to pay a creditor or collection agency, be certain to write the term "post-dated check" in large letters on the check. Otherwise it may clear the bank and they will do nothing about it afterwards.

26. If you are attempting to settle or delay payment to a creditor due to an inability to pay, it is wise not to mention martial problems as a source of your financial problems. Acceptable problems include loss of job, medical bills, etc. Martial problems tend to alert them to an upcoming divorce and they may file legal collection procedures sooner than they normally would.

27. Regardless of what they say, most collection agencies or retailers will not take a debtor to court unless it is a fairly large debt. Court fees, attorneys, and time is expensive and court settlements do not necessarily collect the money if the person is unemployed, has no assets or is a professional deadbeat.

28. If a collection agent or creditor does sue you, he may use a trick called inconvenient venue, meaning he will file in a court as far as possible from you. He needs to have a branch business in this city to do it but if he can file in the county and far from you, it makes it difficult for you to appear at the courthouse to defend yourself.

29. Collection agencies normally charge 50% of any monies collected to the creditor. Therefore, creditors try to avoid collection agencies except when no other avenue of collection seems available.

30. Some creditors will establish their own "collection agency" which is no more than an in-house office using separate stationery.

31. Although not etched in stone, collection agencies will not generally sue for less than $250 or less than $1,000 to $1,200 if they feel you are capable of providing some sort of passable defense.

32. Collection agencies will often settle for a small percentage of the debt in return for listing the account as closed or paid, especially if they see you have a reasonable defense and/or you have no assets or income that can be easily seized or garnished.

33. Even though a debt is paid off, if it is overdue it will be listed on your credit report with a notation "paid off after write-off" or something similar. It does not disappear from the credit report automatically.

34. Bank cards like payments as soon as possible. Normally a reminder notice is sent out 10 - 20 days after the first notice of payment. However, they will allow 90 - 120 days before they actually cancel the card or turn it over to a collection agency or institute other legal action.

35. Bank card companies will normally try to contact you by phone 60 days after an account is due if payment is not forthcoming.

36. It is possible to ask an issuing company to suspend your credit card for six months or so until you pay off the amounts owed them in a series of payments. This sometimes prevents negative credit reports and returns the card to you that otherwise would have been cancelled.

37. It is also sometimes possible to suspend payments to a creditor by giving them a reasonable excuse and asking for a reasonable delay. This is only possible if they feel you are going to pay it off and are not going to disappear nor require them to institute expensive legal collection actions.

38. Approximately one-half of all savings and loan institutions that offer secured credit cards are located in the state of California.

39. Credit inquiries, whether you open an account or not, remain on your record for one year under normal circumstances. Used car dealers, boat dealers, RV dealers, anyone who offers to check your credit over the phone or run a free credit check, will establish a notation on the credit report of a credit check run and no credit applied. More than a couple of these in any period is decidedly negative and you should consider writing the company and saying you did not apply for credit there, especially if they have been run without your permission, and ask the credit reporting agencies to remove these from your file.

40. Rather than apply for an expensive T & E card, especially if you are unsure of your credit status in this higher strata of plastic, apply for a gold Visa or Master-charge. These cards have the same high limits as T & E cards, are accepted in many of the same places, do not require the annual fee, and allow you to pay off the balance in installments rather require payment in full than at the beginning of each month.

41. When you apply for a credit card, if you write self-employed, some credit reporting agencies will list you as unemployed.

42. TRW has a policy of 21 working days to receive or reconfirm disputed information on their credit reports.

43. If you are having a temporary problem paying your bills, it is often better to pay the smaller bills thereby shortening the list of the number of people you owe and let the larger creditors wait a month or two or possibly even three. This generally means you will have a better chance of keeping a positive credit history as the large creditors will not run in the reports until this period has passed.

44. Oil companies generally do not maintain any security forces. Their philosophy is that it's less expensive to absorb losses and bad debts than it is to pay legal fees for skiptracing and collection.

45. If you have a bad record with a finance company, it generally will not be reported to a credit reporting agency. You should not list finance companies on credit applications.

46. Finance companies, do share information with other finance companies and will make your file available to creditors if specifically requested to do so.

47. In areas where banks are competing for credit cards, it is possible that a card may be issued on the basis of job earnings or job history alone with no additional credit history necessary. Generally these are cards with smaller limits, but they are still credit cards and count toward building and maintaining your credit history.

48. There are enough credit cards issued in the United States to give one to every person over the age of 18.

49. There are over 25,000 different credit cards currently available.

50. American Express will sometimes issue cards to college students before they graduate. They like the student to be a college senior who is about to graduate and is probably going to get a job soon that pays a fairly decent salary.

Requirements for this student card are considerably looser than for the normal American Express card. You can write American Express Company, American Express Plaza, New York, New York 10004, and ask for an application to see if you qualify.

51. If you have a Visa or Mastercharge, (even a secured card) and you have a poor credit history, there are some stores that offer "instant credit." Often you can make a couple of purchases at the store, flash your Visa or MasterCard, fill out an application and be issued a temporary store credit card. They may run the application through and revoke this later on, but they may not, in which case they will mail you a permanent card from the store. This is a trick used for rebuilding credit.

52. If a married couple have credit problems and the loans or cards are primarily in the husband's name, sometimes the woman can apply for new credit using one of the methods we've detailed here to generate quick credit in her maiden name. She can then apply for cards to be issued to her husband and no credit check will be run on him nor on her married name (which is not listed).

This sometimes works for friends as well as spouses.

53. It is often possible to get a secured credit card from a savings and loan even when its located on the other coast by writing them and enclosing a certified check or money order for a deposit, preferably at least in the amount of $2,000.

54. Using a credit bureau for illegitimate purposes is punishable by up to a $5,000 fine and a year in jail.

55. TRW utilizes over 20,000 different sources for input to their credit files and generates over 130,000,000 credit history reports to subscribers every year.

56. For an additional $18, Bank of America's bank cards allow you to access legal advice by simply making a phone call.

57. States which enforce a low interest ceiling on bank credit cards, are: Arkansas, Connecticut, Texas, and Washington.

58. Banks in low interest states traditionally reject about 50% of all card applicants in order to keep their write-offs and non-payment incidents low.

59. Banks maintain credit card loss reserve funds. Once these funds are depleted any particular bank will immediately stiffen the requirements to procure a credit card.

60. Credit card consumers are divided into three groups by the credit card industry: revolvers (those who make the minimum amount possible each month), average (those who pay the bill off one month and pay the minimum the next month), and convenience users (those who always pay the bill in full incurring no interest charges).

61. Twenty-five percent of the card holders in the United States freely admit they have no idea of how much interest they pay on their credit card balances.

62. Trans Union maintains a hawk file which is a data base containing social security numbers, addresses, and phone numbers that have been or are fraudulently used on credit applications. This service is accessed over a million times a month by customers at no charge.

63. Credit unions are a possible source of low-cost bank credit card.

64. Many banks will increase the limit on their cards to $5,000 or $10,000 at the request of the customer. This entails no charge and gives one the same high credit

limit that a gold or other premium card would offer.

65. American Express will contact a merchant or retailer with whom you have a dispute and act as an intermediary. They prefer phone calls rather than letters. The toll-free number for customer service is 800-528-4800.

66. Even if a merchant or retailer has a policy of no refunds - no exchanges, a consumer can legally dispute and win any reasonable claim if the purchase is made on a credit card. For this reason, if there is any suspicion of an up-coming problem with the service, transportation company or merchant, one should pay with a credit card and not with cash or a check.

67. When you dispute a charge or merchandise purchase on a single point sale card, or a card issued by a retailer, it is the retailer himself that will arbitrate the dispute. It is preferable in lieu of any possible charge-back requests to use a bank card.

68. Gold, platinum, and other premium plastic generally set a minimum income of $35,000 per family unit before cards are issued.

69. American Express gold card users can cash checks up to $5,000 instead of the normal $1,000 limit by going to a American Express offices.

70. It generally takes three to five days to replace a lost or stolen credit card with the exception of some premium cards which will do an emergency replacement in two days or less.

OWN A BANK

Tired of being turned down for credit? Unamused at the comments on credit reports and credit card rejection slips? Looking for a career in high finance or daytime TV? Don't want to become a bartender or enter the high paid world of computer programming or secretarial school? Like a say in whether you can borrow money and how much at what rates?

There's a simple answer to all these questions. Yes, the C.E.P. self-help program will help you become the president of your very own bank. For a small fee and two weeks of your time. . .

All kidding aside, it is possible and in many cases viable to start one own's bank. You do not have to be named Dow, Rockefeller or Reagan in order to take advantage of the banking laws in the United States. How would one go about founding one's own bank and assuring a place in the annals of financial history?

In the first place, it will not be called a bank. It'll be called a credit union, but don't let the change in nomenclature throw you. A credit union can do many of the same things a bank can do including issue credit cards, loan money, open insured savings accounts, allow profit sharing, pay salaries to employees, issue mortgages, even open checking accounts.

As one might suspect, there are a number of rules and regulations and a fist full of paperwork governing any sort of financial institutions in this country. Credit unions basically require seven people on the board of directors, you and six of your close friends and an initial commitment of 200 people who will invest in the credit union itself.

With 207 people you can actually begin your own bank.

If you are seriously interested in starting a credit union, I suggest you write the National Credit Union Administration, 2025 M Street N.W., Washington, D. C. 20456 and ask them for both the regional office serving your area as well as information they have on startup of credit unions. You might also inquire about the name and address of the office that handles state charters of credit unions in your individual state.

Once you get this address, contact the office and ask for information on starting your own credit union. Most offices will gladly send you brochures, regulations, requirements and exactly what you need to begin your own credit union.

In addition to the 207 people required, there are certain financial reserves and financial obligations that differ from state to state which must be met. The National Credit Union Association will actually help you form a credit union if you can come up with the minimum requirements. Your credit union (your bank) can of course, approve your credit, loan you money, employ you and whatever else is necessary.

It should be pointed out that financial proprietary is required in the United States and the jails are full of people who decided to have some fun with their bank's money. This is not an invitation to fraud nor do we suggest you engage in any sort of illegal activity. However, a legal credit union can be an interesting way to not only improve one's credit but improve one's life.

CREDIT CRIMES

THE CURRENT CROP OF UNCATCHABLE CRIMES

CREDIT CARD CRIMES

In this section we are going to examine the various ways in which credit cards are used fraudulently and for illegal gain. I want to point out that credit card crime ranks as close to the perfect crime as any type of crime can. Less than one in one hundred is prosecuted or even followed up by the authorities and yet, it is one of the most prevalent and profitable types of crime in the world today.

The reasons for this phenomena are simply that the laws or lack of laws actually favor the card holder in an attempt to prevent any infraction upon his privacy or liability. The retailer or other merchandiser is essentially responsible for the credit card transaction at his own risk with very few safeguards built into the system.

We're going to look at the top credit card crimes from two different standpoints - those that are operable strictly from the user's or criminal's standpoint and those that are done from a merchant's standpoint or at least with the cooperation of a retailer or merchant. These are two separate categories of crimes.

We'll also detail the steps that can be used to prevent these crimes as well as what merchants and retailers should look out for in credit card transactions.

Remember even counting just Visa and MasterCard, the credit universe is so vast that 17,000 banks issue Visa cards and 16,000 different banks issue MasterCards. It becomes almost impossible to follow up on any single transaction. In fact, the banks themselves discourage prior clearance or checking except when it is done automatically by computer or by a third guaranteeing party because they simply do not have the personnel to handle the phone calls for transactions generated by one of their credit cards. As a result, most merchants do not even bother to verify the simplest information on the card.

This leads us to the first group of crimes, probably the most common type of credit card crime in the country. This particular crime was thought to be made popular, if not invented, by a California gang, once attributed by the California State Attorney General, as the remnants of the Charles Manson gang. This gang rummaged through trash bins behind department stores, restaurants and other businesses, for the carbons that are normally sandwiched in a credit card charge slip. Once in possession of these carbons, the gang had the name of the credit card holder and the number of the credit card plus the expiration date. This is all the information required to complete many mail and phone transactions.

At this point a member of the gang would call up and order various types of fenceable merchandise, preferably liquid items such as rare coins, gold, or stamps. These were then sent to addresses of friends, mail drops, or in some cases, the gang would actually rent blank offices, and put up a phony placard outside with company and personnel's names on it. Then these non-existent personnel would receive a steady inflow of merchandise for the next few weeks before the gang would move on to more virgin territory.

This process has become somewhat more sophisticated in the last few years as retailers are now advised by most credit card companies to turn over the carbons of the credit cards to the customers themselves eliminating the possibility of someone digging them out of the trash or finding them on the floor or taking them from a drawer. Many credit card holders are becoming wise to this scam and will ask for the carbons. Some credit card charge slips are carbonless, thereby eliminating this step entirely.

However, the same information can be derived from a number of other sources. Often a person working in a bank or credit agency is bribed or coerced into working with other members of a ring and the numbers and imprinted information are gotten from the inside. In the past, computer hackers have gone directly into computers and extracted this information.

Order forms can be often gotten from mail order companies or other large retailers which contain the same information in trash bins and other easily accessible areas. Monthly statements can be intercepted in the mail or in a customer's mail box. The card can simply be observed by someone while it is in use or a retail clerk can simply make duplicate notes of credit card numbers, names and expiration dates.

Under the existing laws, the actual credit card holder is not liable for misuse of his card. He simply has to issue a request for a charge back from the credit card company stating he did not order the merchandise and it's up to the merchandiser to prove he did. This is costly, time consuming and rarely attempted. Local police departments don't have the personnel or the time to try and track down this type of small-time, one shot credit card fraud even though it may add up to millions of dollars worth of merchandise being effectively stolen in a short period of time.

The procedures to counteract this type of criminal activity from a large mail order company's standpoint, are time consuming and difficult, but some companies are finding it worthwhile to employ some of these tactics as their losses are becoming staggering.

In the first place, many companies depend on the hot list sent out by the credit card companies. This is a list of stolen cards or misused numbers. This is ridiculous. The list is out of date and really would catch only the most amateur credit card thieves. Anyone who has any sense will only run a card for a short period of time and then abandon it.

The first four digits of a MasterCard or Visa card are called the BIN or Bank Identification Number. These four digits are a code which shows which bank in the United States actually issued the card. It is possible for companies to buy a book of BIN number cross references that list each bank's address and phone number and the number of the cards they issue. This book is expensive, almost $1,000.

Banks do not encourage this procedure but by law must follow through if asked to do so. If a mail order company has a BIN number book, they will ask the customer for the issuing bank. They will also ask for the billing address on the credit card. The first step in the procedure then is simply to cross reference and see if the issuing bank given by the attempted buyer is actually the bank that issued the credit card. If it is, there's a good chance the card is valid as this information is difficult to come by.

The second step, which most retailers do not bother with unless it is justified by a large purchase, is to actually call the bank and ask if this credit card is held by Mr. John Doe and billed to this address. The bank will take the time to look up the transaction and verify this information with the merchandiser.

Even if a BIN directory is used, the fact that the buyer knows the name of the issuing bank is considered enough proof to go ahead with the sale. Of course, there is nothing to stop people who fraudulently use credit cards from buying a BIN directory and having this information on hand. It's possible to give separate billing and shipping addresses so there is no quick method of following up this information and finding the credit card user if the bank is actually called.

Some retailers will go even a step farther and ask for the phone number of the person ordering the merchandise. Although they will not usually tell you this when they ask, it means they are going to call back and verify that you did indeed order merchandise with your credit card. The ways crooks get around this are to simply have a phone installed someplace in a fake name in a small apartment, use it for a while and then abandon it. Or by using a phone and a forwarding service where a number is automatically forwarded to another number which cannot be traced. Then the original phone, located at an answering service or buried in someone's apartment, can be abandoned with no trace as to the forwarding number.

Another possibility is for the retailer to simply call information or check the phone directory to see if the person is listed at the address given. There's no law that says you have to be listed in a phone book to buy something, but the retailer may refuse this transaction at this point if he feels it is fraudulent use. It's also a wise move for anyone using a fraudulent card to look up the card holder's address and phone or at least have one with the same name and phone so if a random check is made with Telco information, it will appear to verify.

In some sales, especially of expensive items, the merchandiser may send the items insured, registered mail, federal express or UPS, which requires a signature on the part of the receiver. This really doesn't do a lot if the card is being used fraudulently and the address is going to be vacated within a few days after ordering the merchandise as there's nothing to come back on. It is simply a first stage protection and provides one more piece of evidence should the crime ever come to light.

SHARE THE WEALTH

Luckily for the would-be crook or fraudulent credit card user, neither the United Parcel Service or the postal service will, under any circumstances, share any information with retail establishments about fraudulent addresses or bad credit card numbers. This makes it easy to accept deliveries from the postal service because a complaint from a marketer or retailer will not stop or even cause surveillance to be put on any delivery route. The post office feels its job is to deliver the mail, through rain, sleet, snow, etc., for large amounts of money and heavy unionized breaks - well, that's neither here nor there - they do feel they are there to deliver the mail and not enforce credit card fraud limits so they will continue to function until ordered by a court or their own security department to stop.

The one exception to this procedure is that on occasion UPS will reveal zip code areas where they feel they have run into the most problem with fraudulent deliveries. These zip code areas are usually located in heavy minority or economically depressed areas.

Let's be honest, they are usually in slums. A marketer will sometimes use this information or even compile his own list and when receiving an order from one of these zip codes will run through more extensive re-enforcement procedures to make sure the order is valid before shipping it.

RETAIL SALES

The second most common method of fraudulent credit card use is when someone makes a purchase of retail merchandise in person with a stolen or lost credit card. The merchandise is then sold to someone else or even returned for cash, where possible, although some stores will only return credit card sales for credit.

Credit cards are obtained in many ways. Many thieves specialize in quickly disposing of credit cards when they are stolen by a pickpocket or a burglar or found by rummaging through someone's briefcase or car glove compartment.

A more interesting method is for the thief to steal the credit card as it is being delivered to the person's house or post box. The problem with this is a follow-up letter always follows each credit card. This is mailed without any or with a different return address on it and with no reference to the credit card company on the envelope. Inside it says, "We mailed you a credit card. If you have not received it by this time, please call us at once." So any good credit card thief will not only steal the credit card, but also will attempt to steal the verification letter, which usually arrives within the week.

In one incident that we personally investigated, a man who worked in the post office specialized in lifting cards as they were being delivered to post boxes and then lifted the follow-up letters later on. Most people will not realize they should have gotten the card for a month or two as they have just applied for it and don't know exactly when it will come or they don't realize their card is going to expire within the month and that a new card is due to arrive. People rarely call the credit card company inquiring about the arrival of a new card until after the expiration of the old card. Credit cards are normally renewed and sent out a couple of months before the old card expires.

Due to the volume of credit card sales today, it is highly unlikely that any clerk is going to remember the physical description of anyone buying something a week after the fact when it comes to light that a fradulent or stolen credit card was actually used for the transaction.

Some of the countermeasures stores can take against this type of transaction are: always check the card closely to make sure it appears to be real, is signed, and has not expired. They also can ask the customer for his home or business phone number. A good crook will always have fakes on the tip of his tongue. It is possible store personnel will take the time to check the directory or information to verify address and phone number, but again, this is extremely rare and there is no law that says you have to be listed.

If the card in question is an American Express card, one should be aware a good clerk can call security at American Express and ask for verification of the customer's name and address and number. American Express is the only credit card company at this writing to take the time and trouble to verify over the phone if a credit card is billed to the same address as the person attempting to make the purchase has given.

The most common countermeasure is to have an electronic terminal which reads the credit card's magnetic strip, the numbers and expiration date when the card is fed into it. Then automatically dials the central computer and verifies that the credit card is still good. A good crook will either use the credit card before it has been reported stolen or watch prior transactions to see at what floor limit the card is checked or if, indeed, the card is electronically verified at all. If it is, he simply avoids that place of business.

Clerks can also be taught to compare the signatures on the driver's license, and on the charge slip against the signature on the card. However, clerks are not trained policemen and anyone who puts a few minutes into it can learn to duplicate someone else's signature well enough to pass an untrained observer's eye. It is also possible to smear the signature on the back of the credit card without arousing too much suspicion.

Some stores also tell the clerks to record all other printed information such as the driver's license number, address, or phone number, on the credit card slip and then the clerk himself must put his initials or number on it so in case of later problems at least the correct clerk can be located in order to answer any questions about the transaction.

RETURNS

Some thieves, once they have a credit card (or even using their own card) will attempt to return stolen merchandise or merchandise simply picked up off the shelf.

In most cases the store will not issue the cash back, but will issue a return on the credit card if it was supposedly purchased on the card. At this point there is a credit plus on the card that can be used to purchase additional merchandise for resale.

Occasionally a thief will purchase counterfeit merchandise. Now this is especially true in major cities where there are people who specialize in making things like phony Rolex watches, or other phony high-ticket items that seem to be the real thing. These can be purchased in bulk and taken back to a store that carries the original and returned for cash. When this doesn't work, a thief will ask for the money back on his credit card as that was how it was purchased. Surprisingly, this works most of the time.

The counter measures are fairly obvious; retail policies must be strengthened to require a receipt, although this still can be breached by a thief who makes a phony receipt or has a compatriot in the store make up a receipt for him but it cuts out the majority of thieves who do not have access to this procedure.

The retailer should be able to retrieve the credit records to indicate the sale was actually made on the card. Most retailers do not bother with this procedure, even on expensive high-ticket items, making it fairly easy for a thief to use this system.

BREACHING THE FLOOR LIMIT

A wise fraudulent credit card user will make as many purchases of resaleable merchandise as possible which are over the floor limit, (usually $50) until the credit limit is reached on the card. At this point any purchase made over the floor limit is going to alert the credit center and they are going to deny it - not that it is a fraudulent card but simply that the credit limit of the individual has been reached.

The credit line is ascertained by assuming the credit card does not have too much on it and making purchases until one is invalidated by the credit center, or by running a credit check using a computer hacker or a friendly merchant to see how much is left on the card.

Once this is reached the thief will often make as many small purchases under the floor limit as possible in the next few days in order to greatly extend the limit of the card without alerting the credit center. This will eventually produce a warning to the credit card holder and then the card will be placed on the hot list.

However, the elapsed time is usually significant enough that many purchases can be made by a good thief or ring of thieves.

SELF INDUCED FRAUD

Often amateur thieves or kids, will simply order merchandise on their own card and then later on claim they never ordered it. It is important to remember that the law does say if you didn't order it, you're not responsible for payment. There are a couple of other things that come into play. First off, if they check with the issuer to make sure it's coming to the right address, the merchant can protect himself by sending the item registered, certified or insured so a receipt has to be signed. If this is done, and then the card holder claims he didn't order the merchandise, he must return the merchandise. You aren't allowed to just simply keep anything because you didn't order it (if you did receive it) if it's over a certain value.

If the merchant calls to verify the order it's a little hard to claim later on that the buyer did not order it. In this case, it's very likely the card holder is going to pay under threat of prosecution and/or could possibly be prosecuted for attempted fraud.

A VARIATION

Another method is for the credit card holder to order on his own card and then simply lie saying he never received the package. This opens a different can of worms and once again places the burden of proof on the merchant. If receipt cannot be proven, there is generally nothing a merchant can do.

Countermeasures include always having the card holder state that he did place the order by phone before shipment (although most companies do not do this) and then shipping it proof of receipt-required. If a merchant does follow those guidelines, he can prove the card holder did indeed receive it or a member of his family did and he is liable for the money or merchandise. If the merchant does not send it with proof of shipment, he can still ask the card holder to sign a postal claim, which is in effect an affidavit that states that the card holder never received the merchandise.

If the card holder will sign this affidavit which is after all just a piece of paper stating that one is telling the truth, the merchant will have to refund the purchase price or replace the item with a new one. If the thief refuses to sign the claim, he can be charged for the item and the merchant will collect.

If the merchant has proof of shipment, he must re-put through the credit card transaction so that he will hold onto the money rather than the bank keeping the money, which is much more subject to pressure from the card holder, until the matter is resolved.

OF CARS AND MEN

With the proper back-up ID, it is easy for a thief to use a stolen or altered credit card, rent a car from a car rental agency, and then resell the car to an unsuspecting party as his own vehicle. There are a number of ways to do this which we are not going to go into entirely here. But suffice to say, the car can be stripped, the parts sold or it is possible to get a completely new legitimate out-of-state title on the car and then turn the car over to a cash-on-the-spot used car dealer or put an ad in the paper, rent an apartment for a short time and sell it from there.

The same technique can be used where the credit card functions as a down payment to buy a car, boat or motorcycle, and then the vehicle is stripped and sold or a fake title produced and the vehicle sold. In this system, although the thief has illegitimately stolen a car, he has really gone to little trouble. He doesn't know anything about picking locks or hot wiring cars, has some time before the rental period or credit card fraud is discovered in order to advertise and sell the car and exposes himself to little risk except for the fact that he will leave his handwriting behind on the various forms he was required to fill out.

The thief would probably have a mail drop at this point to send any papers to and/or an answering service.

ADDRESS TRICKS

Another common hustle has to do with the billing and shipping addresses on credit cards. The thief starts off with the basic billing information obtained from a carbon copy of a credit card receipt or a clerk, from a friend who has gone into computers and pulled out numbers and expiration dates of current cards. Once he has this information he orders something that requires delivery and has the merchandise sent to a buddy.

Now this sounds like a sure way of getting someone else in trouble, but this isn't the case. The way the law reads now, it is the responsibility of the merchant to prove that the person received the merchandise and did actually order it. If he cannot prove this, the person is not responsible for payment.

It's as simple as that. The credit card company will issue a charge back and subtract it from the merchant's bank account without the hassle.

Normally the thief orders several expensive items and has them sent to friends at other addresses. The friends accept delivery.

These items are often sent non-registered, no signature required upon delivery.

One trick often employed is if the items are to be sent by a federal express or UPS to simply put a note on the door with a phony signature saying the driver can leave the packages if no one is home. The signature has nothing to do with the person on record at the address so it can easily be denied later.

Once the person is billed and the real card owner says he never ordered the merchandise, the delivery addressed person may be questioned. He simply responds that he doesn't remember a package coming like that, and if it had, it would have sent it back to the original company since he didn't order it. That's the end.

Unless someone can prove he did accept delivery and kept the package (which he didn't, of course) nobody pays except the merchant. The merchant is generally believed to be guilty unless proven innocent.

Some less experienced thieves, may use their own credit cards in this manner and have the merchandise delivered to a friend and then claim they never ordered it. This does work and will result in a charge back to the merchant. The person will not pay for the merchandise. However, doing it more than once or twice is bound to create an enormous amount of suspicion and could result in further action being taken, such as a stakeout or registered letters. This is not generally considered wise by anybody who is at all professional.

VARIATIONS ON A THEME

A slightly more sophisticated approach to the idea of one person ordering with a stolen number and another person accepting delivery, can be done with only one person, although it's often done by gangs, using a number of numbers at one time.

This trick is simply to order the merchandise and have it delivered to an empty building. If it is sent by mail or there is a note on the door to the delivery company, the merchandise will usually be left at the building as instructed. The thief, of course, simply stakes out the building and picks up the merchandise after it's been delivered by the post office or delivery service.

This act is extremely hard to trace and there's often no countermeasures.

It's possible to have the orders sent to an empty building or empty apartment and then go to the local post office and fill out a forwarding address card to this address.

These cards usually last for about six months at a time and will result in the post office automatically forwarding any packages that arrive to the new address without leaving any notice on the door where this occurred.

This method has the added safety feature that once the forwarding address runs out, many post offices will discard this information so there is no trace as to where the package was actually delivered.

The follow-up delivery address is normally a mail drop or safe house or some other location that cannot be traced a few months later.

It is also possible to employ a mail drop for a month or so and then file a forwarding change of address at the mail drop. Once the receiver is gone every layer has to be uncovered, making it that much harder for investigators to trace down anything or make any sense of the transactions. This is especially true when several people fill out the forms on various ID's and phony names are used to complicate matters.

The negative side of tricks using the post service is the fact that a good merchant may check with the card holder to see if he ordered the merchandise and/or if the address checks out with the issuing bank. If it's been ordered through the post office and/or delivered by the post office, postal inspectors can be called into the case and they are sometimes more diligent than the average federal inspector who's deluged with credit card fraud cases. Inspectors will watch the mail going to an address, hold up the mail and demand one come in and pick it up.

A further countermeasure involving the post office department is for the merchant in question to make a postal claim to retrieve the value of the shipment. This will only work if the shipment was insured and the postal inspectors verify there was a fraudulent address or apparent fraud involved in the receiving of the merchandise. Most merchants do not bother to insure their merchandise and this really has no relevant bearing on the thief's outlook except for the fact that the postal inspectors will be called in.

DOUBLE YOUR PLEASURE, DOUBLE YOUR FUN

The way the system works right now a credit card holder, either fraudulent or legitimate, can protest any particular charge in two different ways.

1. By writing or calling the merchant and claiming he never received the item or he returned the item or he never ordered the item, all of which will require the merchant to return his money.

2. Then contacting the bank or issuing institution of the Visa or Mastercharge and giving the same story.

Under the present system there are no central cross referencing facilities to show that both chargebacks have been issued.

In other words, it is extremely easy for someone to return a piece of merchandise, ask the company for their money back and also ask the bank for their money back. This produces a double charge back so they have made money and returned the item or even kept it saying they never received it. They also have been paid back for it twice.

To stop this merchants must work closer with issuing banks or with their own bank to make sure money is not removed without immediate notification. He should check to see that this has not happened before issuing charge backs.

GUILTY AGAIN UNTIL PROVEN INNOCENT AGAIN

Issuers of credit cards (banks and other financial institutions) usually allow charge backs for an extended period of time after the initial purchase has been made (a year is about the average). This is up to nine months after the original record has been destroyed by the bank. They will still allow a charge back to the merchant's account to pay a card holder who claims he never received or didn't order the original merchandise.

Some banks will actually go as long as five or six years still allowing charge backs against the company simply on the word of the purchaser.

An interesting sidebar is that in a retail setting if a merchant posts their refund policy on the wall where a customer can see it, it is valid and will be allowed in court.

However, if a mail order or telephone order company posts a non-refund policy or offers a XX-day back money guarantee, this is totally invalid (at the time of this writing) and is simply a convenience to try and dissuade people for asking for charge backs.

The charge back policy is up to each individual bank or institution who, even though the retailer has a set policy will issue a charge back, charge the retailer and refund the money to the customer for up to six years after the purchase. This makes it easy for a thief to come back at a later date and recoup money for merchandise that he's long since resold using his card or other cards.

Countermeasures to this (at the moment) are almost nil although it is expected courts will resolve this dilemma in the not too distant future, possibly in favor of the merchant.

AND OVER AGAIN

If a fraudulent credit card user finds success in ordering from a company either in person or by mail, he may reuse the same technique at the same company. Logically it infers that security in regards to plastic money is extremely lax and he has a very good chance of getting away with it more than once. This can become quite a source of income for some people. They can take the same company over and over again for months until the fraudulent sale finally makes it through the bureaucracy of their credit card or sales security system.

This is an extremely draining procedure for any merchant as you can imagine and the countermeasures are obvious. A merchant should maintain his own file of fraudulent user numbers and addresses.

Let's face it - computers are cheap. Every clerk should have to get approval from the firm's own security center, which includes checking and cross-checking the files. Every card should be run through the electronic verification machine or if a floor limit is breached, a phone call should be made, the BIN directory should be used, and so on.

In most establishments this simply does not occur and plastic thieves walk off well and happy.

MAIL ORDER FOLLOW THROUGH

While there is the "code 10" enforcement procedure covering fraudulent credit card transactions wherein the card and/or the thief are to be appre- hended, most mail order or telephone retail order companies do not subscribe to this procedure simply because they do not handle the actual credit cards.   Even if they check and realize the number is hot or incorrect, they will not usually follow through with any attempt to apprehend the user.

Who says there's no such thing as a perfect crime?

In the first place the companies are out nothing. They simply don't fill the order or send a notice saying the credit card is no longer valid. The crime, if any, committed at this point is going to be something like attempted fraud or attempt to defraud a merchant which is probably a misdemeanor. No police department wants to follow it up over four states. It just isn't worth the effort. Mail order or counterfeit attempts are by their very genre safer than "in person" attempts that leave an impression with a clerk or get the perp apprehended on the spot.

The counter to this is for credit issuing banks and retailers to develop tracking systems so they can find people who are misusing these cards or numbers and attempt to follow through and prosecute the people. There are a couple 24-hour credit card hot lines which we've mentioned elsewhere which can curb multiple offenders. Any good mail order firm or retailer should join these associations and use the lines.

At the very least, retailers should develop cross-reference fraud lists with names, addresses, phone numbers and credit card numbers so they can instantly tell if a card has burned one of their competitors. After all they are not competitors when it comes to losing money due to fraudulent transactions. Many also would be wise to use the BIN number directory and a directory that lists prisons to make sure card transactions are not being sent to a federal or state institution.

Credit card issuing banks probably have the greatest consumer data banks in the world on consumers. Yet at this point they don't cross-reference or connect their computers. They don't talk to each other as much as they should in order to prevent fraud.

Under the credit card act people who use fraudulent, altered or stolen cards more than one time and purchase things worth $1,000 or more, can be convicted of mail order fraud. At this time the company has to convince the law enforcement agency to go out and do the actual search by swearing they are going to prosecute. This takes an enormous amount of time and hassle for a small loss, or in the case of an early identification, for no loss at all. As such most of these long distance transactions are extremely safe for the fraudulent user.

DOUBLE INDEMNITY; INMATE FRAUD

Within the last month as I write this, a New Orleans bank sent almost 100 credit cards to a group of customers, who were verified by its computer to have steady jobs and noteworthy records. That is to say they had not run up any bad credit within the last three years and were employed.

This is most accurate. They were all inmates of the Angola State Prison. Needless to say, the cards were used to order things that were not necessarily paid for.

This sounds like a very odd situation, but in fact, is quite common. There's a number of variations but generally it is quite possible for a prison inmate to get a credit card. In the first place, many prisons now do not say they are prisons on the return address of an outgoing envelope. Some will go as far, especially minimum security or farms, as to let the inmate actually put a "suite" number on return mail.

Banks or bank clerks do not have the time nor are they cognizant of what a prison number looks like anyway, so this often slips by undetected, and banks will issue on previous credit history, made up credit history and send cards directly to the prison.

Often the prisoners will form a group or a ring and use the cards to order merchandise. The merchandise may be sent directly to the prison depending on the type of installation or sent to a friend or an accomplice on the outside who resells it and splits the profits with the inmate.

This has been made easier in the last few years as medium, minimum and even maximum security prisons now allow almost completely unregulated use of a pay phone by inmates. A few years ago this was unheard of in prison populations.

In fact, many prisons regulated outgoing phone calls by inmates to one or two a year, usually on Christmas or Easter only to relatives. These days are long gone and by the judicious use of return addresses on outgoing mail and phone numbers, a prisoner may order a card, get it verified, order material by phone and send it to anyone.

As one might suspect, prisons are full of people who know how to regulate the credit card system, having done so many times in the past. They can usually convince new inmates to take part in these schemes, thereby broadening their influence.

One variation is to have an accomplice on the outside who works for a telemarketing company, is in a retail position or works in a bank where he can get credit card numbers, feed them to a prisoner on the inside who then makes the calls ordering the merchandise and sending it to other accomplices.

As odd as it may seem, this is a fairly difficult practice to detect and stop. In the first place, there's really only one book that lists prison addresses and phone numbers and the way the numbers are written up as to alert credit card issuing companies and/or retailers that this order is indeed for an inmate of a penal institution. This directory costs several hundred dollars and most people do not have it nor do most people take the time to use it except large mail order companies who sell expensive items and have learned this is necessary.

Secondly, sometimes it's hard to prove who got the material once it gets in the prison and most local sheriffs, police and district attorneys, are very hesitant to investigate and/or prosecute this type of crime.

Basically this means taking a prisoner who's already doing time, out of the prison, into a court room at tax payer's expense, to try to convict him of something. He may be doing a long sentence for a more serious crime to which a judge is probably not going to add any time for the rather minor (in the eyes of the law) fraudulent use of a credit card. It's difficult to get local authorities and often prison authorities to prosecute this type of crime, or even look for the merchandise.

CONGRATULATIONS, YOU MAY HAVE ALREADY WON . . .

Some pro card thieves actually use a variation of the old Arthur Murray dance studio technique, "If you can answer this question, 'Who was the first president of the United States', you may have won five free dance lessons at your local Arthur Murray Studio."

The perp calls up targets, usually at random or from a list he's gotten of mail order buyers, (which means most of them have credit cards). He offers an incentive because they "want to introduce people to their new program," they are going to give them some item (it's best not to use the word "prize"). Make it part of an advertising gimmick. One can offer something worth $10 - $50 for a $5 handling charge only. There's no additional charge on the card, there's no additional money to pay.

They will receive a copy of your catalog should they want to order anything else at wonderful discount prices, on and on. Could you please have their credit card number for billing the postage and handling fee?

The caller needs expiration date of the credit card and, if it is carried one step farther, the issuing bank and billing address of the credit card. This supplies all the information needed.

The merchandise is never sent and all the information is at hand to turn around and order items from a legitimate retailer. The thief has all the information needed to pass a BIN number verification or the billing address process.

This is a very safe system and is hard to trace down and stop, much less recover any of the money or merchandise involved.

Some perps will even go one step farther and rent a mail drop, using a phony ID. They make up catalogs offering ridiculously low prices or use fliers which offer something free, mail them out to selected lists of people interested in this sort of thing (a free coin, stamp, knife, etc.) making the offer too good to pass up.

The customers are to receive an item worth $20, $30, or $40 for only a $5 postage and handling charge.

This scheme will attract a large number of credit card orders. It's best to indicate you prefer credit cards or you'll get a lot of people sending $5 cash. This does constitute postal fraud and will bring in the postal inspectors, who as we've pointed out, are often more diligent than the police department credit fraud inspectors. But it is still done and results in large numbers of credit cards, names, numbers, expiration dates, issuing banks and whatever else is required on the form for the targets to receive their free gift.

This is a very difficult crime to counter.

CASH ON THE SPOT

One of the more lucrative methods of using a stolen or counterfeit credit card, which may or may not require fake backup ID, is to go to a bank who will honor the credit card up to a certain cash limit, and get cash on the spot. In banks and ATM machines, it is possible to get $200-$500 on Visa or MasterCard as an advance that is paid back by the usual credit card billing method.

It's also possible to get a line of credit, which means one can actually walk in and get an instant loan for $2,000 to $20,000 depending on the card and the bank. Needless to say in the latter case, you'd better be armed with a lot more information about the supposed credit card owner. The bank is going to ask for job references and possibly check them out. They are going to check every bit of information the thief gives them against their own records. A good thief has either created a paper person in advance, has run complete credit checks or has an accomplice so all the information he gives on the credit card owner's background will be valid.

A variation on this theme is to take the card to a non-bank that still give cash on credit cards. There are a number of networks set up now at places which need cash, notably casinos, sometimes at race tracks and even from machines at airports, although the latter is usually limited to American Express cards. These agencies are established to allow someone who has caught betting fever to continue to play although he has no money.

A most ingenious situation.

The way this is works is by running the credit card through the normal verification process. These days it is usually the electronic verification machine and if it comes up o.k., issuing cash on the spot to the credit card holder.

Note this goes on the credit card cash limit just as if a purchase had been made. In other words, instead of buying a vido cassette tape recorder, one is simply buying cash which lets one go back and lose it at the casino. These instant cash transactions work quite well and are difficult to trace.

Most use no more than their own hot sheets or verification network because they do not have the time or want to spend the effort to chase down BIN numbers, security numbers, and so on for a $200 to $500 cash advance. This is one of the more popular uses of stolen credit cards by hookers, pimps, or pickpockets, people who will get the cards in circulation even before they have been noticed or reported stolen and recover instant cash from them.

Remember, in this situation there's no fronting or selling of hot goods. The thief has actually gotten cash for the card which can be discarded when the limit is reached or sold to some other unwary thief who will then do something stupid with the card.

TRASH COVER

One of the FBI, CIA and one must assume the KGB's favorite methods of gaining information is not an esoteric phone tape, room bug or laser-powered bugging device, but something known as a trash cover. This simply means that some poor s.o.b., probably a new agent, is assigned to go through the trash on pickup night outside of a subject's house, apartment or business.

As we've pointed out it has become fairly common knowledge that going through the trash bins behind stores or restaurants can produce credit card numbers although this effort has been negated on some occasions by carbonless credit card receipts and by awareness on the part of management.

If someone knows that most credit card companies send out their statements near the first or the end of the month, it is a fairly simple matter to go through a credit card user's garbage at that time and find statements from the credit card company. This gives the thief the credit card number, expiration date, credit limit, the billing address, the bank who issued the card, everything but the signature, which is often not necessary.

Yes, sometimes being a thief is a dirty business, but someone has to do it.

SCOTCH TAPE NAMES

It's possible for a third party to get credit card embossed information, i.e., names, number, and expiration date by sureptitiously placing a piece of scotch magic tape on the inner surface of an embossing machine used by a gas station or store. This is especially true of the older style embossing machines which had a press down feature rather than the type that employ a roller to emboss carbonless receipts. Once the scotch tape is in place, it will usually go unnoticed by the clerk who places a card and receipt paper in and presses down or rolls through, without checking the underside of the embossing machine.

The scotch tape can then be lifted off and will produce a faint, but legible impression of the data run through the card machine. This technique is especially useful in fairly low traffic areas where one clerk may be doing more than one job such as a hostess in a restaurant or a gas station attendant who must attend to the cars as well as the credit card machine.

Money may be locked up in a drawer but very few people think to lock up the credit card machine as it's just another piece of machinery.

TO SIGN OR NOT TO SIGN

There are a couple ways in which the signature strip on the back of a card becomes very important in fraudulent credit card transactions. The first is when a card holder does not sign his card, thereby letting a thief, either on purpose (because the thief's an accomplice) or due to his own carelessness, sign in his own handwriting thereby verifying any signature he signs on the receipt.

Many restaurants and stores now will ask you to sign the bottom of the receipt when you pay merchandise or services. What they are doing is comparing this with the signature on the credit card itself, the most basic of all security procedures.

A few of our staff, just for the hell of it, left their credit cards unsigned to see when this would be detected. The average number of transactions accomplished ranged between 15 - 25 before some clerk noticed the card was unsigned.

One staff member had an American Express card go one full year from expiration date to expiration date without ever signing the card or being asked to. He made an average number of purchases with the card and had billings every month.

If the unsigning gets noticed, the place of business will usually ask the user to sign the card in front of them, which is no problem and matches up very nicely with the "high security" technique of having the person sign the receipt.

A slight variation on this trick is to simply paste over the signature on the card with carefully cut white tape, which appears to match the original signature strip or by making a cutout stencil masking the remainder of the back of the card and spraying over it with fast-drying white paint. Either technique allows the thief to put his new signature on the stolen card.

The countermeasure is to erase a slight corner of the strip and see if the word "void" or something similar appears as it does on Visa and Mastercharge and most other cards. It will not on an altered card.

One can also run a finger over the strip to see if it feels like there is a raised layer that might peel off or even attempt to peel it off. The signature strip will never peel off a real card.

Another countermeasure is for the clerk to ask for back-up ID. The problem with this is it tends to insult honest customers. For some reason they feel, especially if they are out to impress a date or their mother, this request implies the restaurant or store thinks they are crooked. Therefore, most establishments will not go to this length to ask for back-up ID.

Any thief with any experience is going to have some kind of back-up ID along for the ride. Even marginal ID will often pass in this situation because of the so-called embarrassment that both the waiter, clerk and credit card holder are going through.

It's also interesting to note that on over 91 percent of all credit cards purchases, clerks or merchants fail to ask for back-up ID. There's no law that says they have to, but after getting stuck a few times, you would think they would.

Even with the cautious nine percent, if the credit card user says, "Gosh, I lost my wallet. Guess I left it in the wash. Jeez, I don't know what happened to my driver's license. It must be in the car," will rarely cause a scene or involve the police. If the customer agrees to put the purchase down until he comes back or in the case of something already consumed as a dinner, offers to pay for it with pocket cash.

That solves everyone's problem.

PICK-UP

Once a thief has a list of numbers or expiration dates, a slight variation on the normal routine of ordering by mail or phone which requires less risk, is to call up a local store and order merchandise - TV's, stereos, radios, something that can be easily resold and is worth the time and effort required - using the numbers and telling the store he will pick up the items at their warehouse.

Many stores will allow this and will o.k. the transaction ahead of time. When the thief arrives to pick up the items, he does not need to show the credit card. In fact, he should not even carry it. It is wise to have backup ID's as they may want to see something when one picks it up but many stores do not even require this. The obvious excuse, if anything goes wrong, is that you're picking it up for a friend.

Another method that has worked in the past, is to have the material picked up by a messenger service for a fee and delivered. It is then delivered to a mail drop, an empty apartment or another place where the messenger can be met. If there's any doubt, the thief will watch the messenger to see if he's followed as he picks up the material. If he is, the entire scheme is simply dropped.

MONEY BY WIRE

Another popular scam is to take a fraudulent credit card: counterfeit, stolen or altered, and arm it with backup ID. Go to Western Union, then telegraph cash to a friend or accomplice or to yourself in another name in another city. It is a simple matter for a person or even the thief himself to go pick up the cash using only a minimal amount of ID. Often Western Union will demand a code word or code phrase to send along with the cash so the person at the other end has to verify they are the receiver.

This method is another easy way to get cash from a credit card without having to resell any merchandise. It requires fairly little exposure and if the card is not listed as hot and not over the credit limit, it will usually be honored by Western Union.

CASH ON THE SPOT: FOREIGN

A variation on the cash-on-the-spot network method is for the thief to take his stolen, altered or counterfeit credit card on vacation with him. A pro takes more than one and simply applies at foreign banks or foreign networks for foreign currency using his credit card as a reference. This will require back-up ID, but has a built in layer of safety because most out-of-the-country banks will not make a long distance phone call, especially considering the time difference involved to verify BIN numbers or original owners' addresses.

In this way it's possible to cash out up to at least the limit of the card and sometimes many times over that because of poor communication facilities or lack of organization that allows them to issue cash and then bill the card company because they know they'll be reimbursed. The thief then takes the foreign currency, buys something, or leaves the country immediately, turning in the money for American currency at a commercial currency exchange.

In many countries the hotel rules and the rules on tourists are much more strict than they are in the United States. A wise thief does not check into a hotel in his own name or a name used on the credit cards because the police tend to keep much closer track of who goes where in foreign countries and many foreign jails are not nearly as much fun as jails in America.

Back up ID's are a must in any of these situations. In other countries many officials will not have access to exact copies of ID's. They may not subscribe to any of the up-to-date services that show what real driver's licenses look like or what government cards look like.

VARIATION ON VACATIONS

It is possible to employ stolen or counterfeit cards in a foreign country to simply buy merchandise. More and more countries are very happy to see that lovely United States issued Visa or MasterCard plastic. After all, if you can't trust someone from the United States, who's obviously rich, who can you trust?

In this case merchandise that can be resold in the states is purchased; i.e., art objects, jewels if possible, or local items that are popular in the states.

Foreign countries may not require backup ID and virtually no foreign merchant will have a BIN directory or access to the bank or original credit card owner. The only countermeasure in this situation is for the merchant to Telex the bank or a security center in the United States. This is an extremely rare, tedious process that requires a lot of time.

I'm certain if one attempted to buy a new Porsche in Germany on a credit card, one would find a Telexed verification in use, however, in most cases merchandise up to $1,000 is not checked out by Telex.

Most foreign merchants have no idea of what correct ID looks like from another country. They are exposed to too many styles and, in some cases, are unable to grasp the concept of each state in America having a different ID. Anything with a picture, any of the various phony ID's being sold on the market with a state name on them (legally sold I might add, through magazines like *Soldier of Fortune)*, are often accepted in foreign countries while they would be laughed at here at home.

REVERSE VACATIONS

In many cases it's much easier to obtain credit cards or credit card numbers in foreign countries because the security systems are not nearly as sophisticated as they are in the United States nor is there as much credit card crime there as here. Older receipts with carbon papers may still be used. The simple trick of going through the trash bin of a fancy, foreign restaurant or large store, gives many numbers, expiration dates and names of foreign credit card holders (non-U.S. credit card holders).

These numbers or cards, if they are stolen or purchased overseas, which makes it fairly easy to bring the cards back into this country (smuggle them through, of course) or just the numbers and make purchases in the U.S. Back- up ID is a help, although not always necessary. Most merchants do not have the sense to ask for a passport to back purchases up (especially a clerk) and will look at a foreign driver's license that says "Kenya" like he knows what it should look like because he's embarrassed to admit he doesn't know if the ID is any good or not, so he'll accept it.

Normally it takes several months for these errorroneous purchases to appear on the credit card holder's statement and at this point the original credit card holder has to go to the police and/or security department; on and on and on.

The chances of catching somebody after this occurs are virtually nil as there is no paper trail left behind. There's simply no way to track somebody down. The clerk is not going to remember anyone's face after time expires.

The countermeasures to this are, of course, to have clerks ask for some ID that he can recognize, demand to see a passport, have access to accurate photos of passports and visa so they know what they are looking for, and to refuse to sell the merchandise if it does not match up.

It is extremely rare to find any store that will train a clerk this thoroughly.

CARD HOLDER CARELESSNESS

Many credit card holders unwillingly and/or unwittinly help credit card thieves by carrying so many credit cards they don't notice if one or two are missing, by storing them in inappropriate places such as glove compartments of cars, by leaving them in jacket pockets. Even after discovery they take too much time to report the loss of any card.

This is compounded by the fact the only amount a card holder is going to be responsible for is the $50, the legal penalty which they are charged if they report the card stolen. Even after charges have been rendered fraudulently on the card, the owner is responsible for only a $50 fine. If they report the card stolen before charges have been incurred, they are not responsible for a cent.

Many issuing institutions do not bother to enforce the $50 fine. It is simply more hassle than it is worth and tends to alienate the card holders. Perhaps they would cancel their checking accounts or other transactions with the bank. Some banks even offer $50 worth of insurance free when you sign up for their credit card. This means not even a $50 penalty is there to deter anyone from being careless or fraudulent with their credit cards.

It is also interesting to note that if the $50 fine is levied, the merchant who got taken receives none of this $50. It simply goes to the bank which in effect lets the bank create a profit on a stolen credit card because they are taking money out of the merchant's account to cover the loss of merchandise and then they make a $50 profit on the theft of the card from the card holder.

Guilty until proven innocent.

Another slight variation on this is that many insurance policies, especially home owners' insurance policies, have a built-in credit card clause. This says you are covered for $200, $500, or $1,000 on any credit card fraud if your card is used in fraudulent transactions. This sounds great except for two items: A. You are legally responsible for only $50 as long as you report the theft. B. This only applies if the card is physically stolen from you - not if the number of the card is copied in any of the manners we've described and used. The number is not your card and therefore does not fall under the insurance company's policy.

TRICKS FROM A TRICK

Although many people consider prostitution a victimless crime (and I'm not here to argue it one way or another), any policemen will tell you that prostitutes are often involved in allied crimes. One of the most popular of which is to go through the John's wallet, coat, or pant's pocket while she has access to them while they are are off and steal ID and credit cards.

This has several advantages over other types of credit card theft. In the first place, if the credit cards are taken by themselves and the money is left in the wallet, the loss may not be noticed until the John goes to use the credit card at some later date as there will have been no apparent tampering.

The prostitute often turns cards over to her pimp or a friend who runs the numbers very quickly or resells the cards on the black market so the numbers are run before they reach the hot sheet. Then the card is disposed of.

Other advantages include that even if they are noticed missing, it is very difficult for a married John or someone in a job with responsibility to go to the police and report how and when the cards were stolen.

The law does say if plastic is reported stolen, liability of the credit card holder is limited to $50. The credit card holder does not have to tell the truth about how they were stolen, he can just simply claim they are missing and make up a story that they were probably stolen at the gym a few days ago when he had his pants in his locker.

The John will often hesitate a few days to report even this version, knowing full well

142

he's only going to be responsible for the first $50. This puts some distance between himself and the prostitute or the act of prostitution, thereby saving himself the trouble of coming up with excuses either for the police or his spouse as to why he was in this particular neighborhood and why he was with this nice, young lady he met on the street corner.

This game flourishes in big cities and many, many, many credit cards are moved in the red light districts of any major city.

The only countermeasures against this are to employ the normal procedures to see if the card is hot listed or use the BIN book to see if the order is legitimate.

There are no real countermeasures specifically that fit this particular crime. The only advice one can give to a credit card holder is if you are going to indulge in the particular form of recreation, keep your pants and wallet in sight at all times. It is common for the girl to induce you to undress in one area and then move to the bedroom giving herself, or more often her pimp or accomplice (who also has a key to the room) a chance to come in unnoticed while you are involved and rifle your pants removing the goodies.

Use common sense.

THE CREDIT CARD AS ID

Another off-played trick by fraudulent credit card users is to obtain checks on someone else's account or open an account with a minimal amount of money. Some banks will actually open an account with $5.00 and a little fake ID. Often this can be non-photo driver's license or by mail obtained photo ID which will sort of pass on its own but will not survive under close inspection.

Then the thieves buy merchandise using a fraudulent credit card or counterfeit credit card to back up their ID. Anyone who has a driver's license, even if it doesn't look quite right or has or a temporary ID that has a major credit card to back it up, obviously is on the up and up.

This involves more than one crime and also leaves a good sample of the thief's handwriting and perhaps some impression of the thief himself at the scene of the crime. However, it's a fairly easy way to generate large amounts of money or buy large amounts of merchandise.

APPROVAL/RENTING

A fraudulent card holder will often find it easier to take something, especially if his image fits what he's trying to buy, on approval. This can be a piece of art, jewelry, a painting, anything that can require the user to see if it fits into his surroundings with promise to pay for the item or return it a day or two later.

It's also possible to rent many things - sporting goods, windsurfers, sail boats, or furniture. Many things do not have serial numbers or require a title. One simply leaves a blank credit card slip with the agent to cover the rent.

In theory, if the renter runs off with the product, the credit card is filled in with the entire price of the product and processed. Remember it is pre-signed and it is blank.

In very few cases will the retailer or rental person bother to check if the credit card is valid as no purchases are being made on it at rental time. In fact, even when it's on an approval, the odds are very slim the credit card will be verified in any form.

Needless to say the person who rented the item or took the item home on approval simply disappears leaving the merchant with a piece of worthless paper and a worthless signature. This scam often doesn't even require backup ID.

Clerks and owners must be taught basic prevention methods: checking BIN books, getting authorization before the item leaves the store and verifying and writing down other ID numbers on the rental slip itself.

FRAUD BY MEMBERSHIP

Here is a rather unusual credit card fraud that has the advantage of not only producing the merchandise at no cost and very little risk to the thief, but actually moving the merchandise at near retail cost rather than having to sell it as hot.

The trick is to form a discount buying club. Chances are you've come in contact with a legitimate discount buying club one time or other in your life. You may have been solicited to join one if you belong to any organizations, clubs, where you work, or by direct mail. The idea of a discount buying club is that buying orders in volume, individual recipients can receive discounts on merchandise.

The selection of merchandise may not be as great as in department stores or normal mail order Sears-type catalogs, but the fewer choices are compensated by the fact there is usually a considerable discount in these types of clubs.

Sometimes enterprising thieves, who have access to credit card numbers, will form their own discount club, find which mail order merchants or even normal over-the-counter merchants, are fairly easy marks for credit card fraud, print up fliers listing the top items they can get from these people offering it at a good discount for cash.

Now the thief recruits people to join his club, sometimes having them pay a membership fee, distributes the fliers and encourages immediate orders.

Once the merchandise orders have been placed, the thief buys the merchandise with the fraudulent credit cards or fraudulent credit card numbers, turns around and delivers it to the club members who have paid cash to the thief for the items in good faith.

This is a very sticky situation because even if the merchandise is eventually located or recovered, the person who bought it did so in good faith from a supposedly legitimate organization. By the letter of the law, the merchandise is stolen and in most countries (with the exception of Switzerland which has a good faith buying law), the merchandise should be returned.

However, this is a very long and tedious process and courts do not always uphold this concept when it is obvious that the person buying the merchandise bought it in good faith and was assured he was buying legal goods.

The thief is nowhere to be found by this time and the club members who have the merchandise are not likely to come forward. This scam is often done in businesses which employ a lot of employees with a heavy turnover. Here one can get a job quite easily (such as a commission sales job) keep the job for a couple weeks while one solicits orders, and even if he's fired from the job comes through on the club, collects his cash and disappears.

This scheme has even been done in prisons. A con sets up the buying club, sells the material to other cons and when the credit card company comes for it, they find the con who set it up used fraudulent numbers and names and had it sent to a "friend." It is almost impossible to prove the other inmates purchased the items knowing they were stolen. This is an interesting variation that works both ends of the deal, very rapidly, very effectively, and does not leave the merchandise sitting around for any length of time.

PAPER PEOPLE

Some enterprising crooks go as far as to create a paper person with a real work and credit history. This is accomplished in a variety of ways.

People simply obtain a credit card number and billing information for a real credit card holder and then apply for other credit cards using the original as a reference source. When this is attempted, the new credit card is always billed to a different address than the original, usually a mail drop.

More enterprising crooks have been known to skip this step entirely and create a credit history for someone who does exist. The simpliest way to do this is to run a credit check on the proposed target. Normally this is done by joining an organization like TRW or other credit reporting agencies or having a computer hacker in the area who has the password (this is much more common than most people suspect) tap into the credit department's data and find out credit history on anyone or by going to a friendly merchant who already belongs to TRW and paying him a small fee to run credit checks on proposed targets.

Once a credit check has been run, especially with a company like TRW, one knows pretty much all the target's credit history, including his place of employment, credit cards already held, his address, and if his credit's good or bad. Once this information is obtained, it's a simple matter to apply for other credit cards in this person's name, listing all the real information with the exception, of course, of the address.

In this manner, the real person with the real credit history, will receive additional cards based on this same credit report as the credit card companies check out the report or check with other credit card companies to make sure he is a good risk.

Once established the new cards will arrive, all ready to go at the phony address. Once a crime has been committed, it is extremely tedious to track down as the person won't know that the card is actually in existence or that charges have been made. He will receive no billing until it goes far enough that the companies who delivered the merchandise begin threatening law suits or turn it over to a collection agency for collection.

At this point, the first step the collection agency or other persons attempting to collect on the account will take is simply to write the phony credit card holder requesting payment. Then they may send a certified letter threatening to sue or a summons to court to the new address. Once it develops further (months down the road) it may go to court or the collection agency may attempt, depending on the state laws, to contact the person at work. Of course, they will contact the real credit card holder since it is his credit card history that has been used. He will deny ordering the card or living at that address.

An investigation will ensue that will consume more months. The real credit card holder will be off the hook since he obviously did not order the card.

Chances of anyone running anything down at this point in an investigation are almost nil.

It's important to note from the credit history which cards the real person already has so the thief does not order the same cards.

It would look suspicious to get a new request from someone who already holds a Visa card or MasterCard from the same establishment. It is possible to get different Visa and different MasterCards from different issuing banks as banks encourage customers to apply for their cards, even if they already hold a similar card from another establishment. This does not raise suspicion, especially if the other establishment's card is listed as a reference.

To further complicate matters, most thieves will have an accomplice fill out the forms or someone they meet in a bar sign so their handwriting does not appear anywhere on the original applications. A good thief will leave no tracks for any law enforcement or collection agency to follow.

In this case the plastic person really does exist. He is simply applying for additional credit he could get under the circumstances. As such, there is no reason to become suspicious or deny this person's application. Some cards are harder to get than others and not every card is an automatic issue. Chances are good, if a person has a good credit history which has already checked out, that any cards he applies for will be issued without question.

Countermeasures for this type of crime are few and far between. If the card is a correctly issued card, it will hold up in a BIN directory, and if the paper person is receiving mail at the mail drop during the period in which he is ordering merchandise, a call to the bank won't even uncover the fraud because any cross reference check will come out positive.

Mistakes occur when the thief gets sloppy or too greedy and holds onto the card too long, using it well past the time common sense would dictate. And as such, runs the card to the ground. This creates a situation where the card appears on hot lists and the bank will no longer verify the card as being safe. This is very rare, especially if the merchandise is ordered by mail or phone and sent to a mail drop. The only way this can be countered is an actual stakeout of the mail drop by federal authorities to apprehend the thief as he picks up the packages.

TIME LIMITS

Banks are required to keep physical checks for six months after their issuance. This is so the federal government, namely the IRS, can catch you in fraudulent activities. Then they are required to keep microfilm or microfiche copies of those same checks for two to five years after the checks go through. As you probably know, by law an individual is required to keep his financial records for five years.

The credit card industry, on the other hand, being a non-regulated industry, has a general rule of keeping credit card records for only three months. This "non-regulated" classification provides huge holes in the security system by only holding each individual transaction record for a short period. If a thief makes charges in several different locations around the country or even the world, files changes of addresses, or uses other methods to generally slow up the system, there's no cross referencing possible because all records will have been destroyed.

This is a huge break for the thief and allows fraudulent orders to be entered over a period of months as long as there's a break in between causing the records to be destroyed.

LETTING YOUR FINGERS DO THE WALKING

It's possible for a bold thief to enter a change of address notice to any merchant of his choice. If you'll recall when you enter a change of address card at the post office they do not ask for ID. One can pick out a merchant who receives a large number of mail order transactions and enter a change of address for that merchant sending all the mail to a blank apartment or to a mail drop that has been secured with no ID or with false ID.

Obviously this cannot go on forever but until it's sorted out, it is possible for the would be thief to receive hundreds or even thousands of credit card charge slips and orders from the firm's customers, which have all the necessary information on the orders to make purchases from other merchants.

There are few counters to this trick. Postal authorities should be aware that they are not delivering to blank addresses, mail drops should be monitored, but they are not.

CHAPTER 13 HEAVEN

It's possible for someone, notice I hesitate to use the word thief in this regard, however, the cumulative results are about the same, to apply for any number of credit cards he or she desires, by establishing credit with a major company such as Visa, Mastercharge, or AE. It becomes simple to apply for additional cards of all varieties. Some individuals have gotten hundreds and hundreds of cards in their own name. People collect cards like other people collect postage stamps or coins.

One type of incident that has occurred during the last years has been that one individual will establish his credit, usually on a legitimate basis. Then he solicits as many credit cards as possible, and runs a maximum credit limit on all cards by buying merchandise, services, tickets, or anything that can be resold. He then conveniently loses his job or finds some excuse and files Chapter 13 bankruptcy.

In this case the individual's possessions are confiscated to pay off the secured debtors. However, in many states if you've homesteaded your house, you will not lose the house itself and there is a set limit on the value of items or salary that can be taken for a Chapter 13 judgment.

We are not advising anyone to do this or purposely exceed their income to the point where they have to file bankruptcy. Should that happen to you, our only advice is to consult an attorney. It is necessary to note filing bankruptcy stays on the record for seven years. You can only file bankruptcy once every 13 years. Some of the sleazier card companies and/or furniture stores, etc. will still extend you credit because they know you can't file again.

During bankruptcy the judge may want to know what's become of the merchandise you purchased. There's no law that says you have to be a good businessman or live your life profitably. By filing bankruptcy you are in effect admitting you've screwed up and the merchandise all went for booze or cocaine or your wife or girlfriend left with most of it. As long as you are not caught selling it out the back door which is illegal, there is really nothing that can be done about payback. This is a simple write-off for credit card companies. It is an uncollectible debt by law and there is really very little stigma attached to bankruptcies any more. <u>Although it is fraud to order merchandise you know you can't pay for.</u>

Many banks now have little signs on the teller's windows or in their checking statements about how going bankrupt is not the answer and can hurt your credit record forever because they are afraid of people doing exactly this.

Many thieves have in the past, created entire paper people, run up huge amounts in their names and then bankrupted the paper person. The alternative is filing their own bankruptcy and then forming a paper person to obtain credit until the regulatory time has passed and the bankruptcy is expunged from one's credit record.

TRAVEL AND ENTERTAINMENT FRAUD BY PHONE

Another scam that has been employed for some time is for the credit card thief, once he's obtained the necessary information, to simply call and order tickets on airlines, for popular sporting events, plays and other expensive performances, pay for them over the phone, then pick up the tickets from a ticket outlet or travel agency.

It is also a simple matter to hire an answering service for a month or two, preferably one that can be rented without showing up in person. Most small answering services will take this type of arrangement.

Then he places an ad in the local paper for a pair of tickets to the Rolling Stones meet the Who. Even though the thief may have 200 tickets, he just advertises four or five. Then sells the tickets legitimately to the people who call. It's also possible to scalp the tickets to any sold out concert by showing up at concert time. This is borderline illegal in itself, this is rarely prosecuted.

Airline tickets are even better. They can be used or turned back in, although many airline companies will only credit the original credit card rather than giving back any cash. What most thieves do, once they have an airline ticket is advertise it in the paper and sell the ticket at a slight discount or simply go to the airport and find people in line trying to buy tickets, approach them in line and explain your mother is having her cataract operation that very day you planned on going to Europe. It's such a drag, but would they like to buy your ticket at a discount, saving them selves several hundred dollars? If they are suspicious they can check to make sure the ticket is good by calling the airline or asking at the counter.

Some airlines discourage this type of sale. The person simply has to walk up and say, "Hi. I'm Joe Schmoo. This is my ticket. Is it a good ticket"?

The airline clerk will be happy to verify it for the actual customer. The credit card fraud is not ascertained until long after the trip is over. There is no way it can be traced back to the person who actually took the trip.

HACKING

It's becoming more and more common for computer hackers to enter data bases surreptitiously. As we have mentioned elsewhere, many hackers have the code words for the various credit agencies around the country and it doesn't take a lot of time and effort for someone to attend the various computer clubs, which are listed in magazines and local universities, and find someone who loves to brag about the fact they have code words to enter these computers.

Other hackers have code words and phone numbers to enter the credit card bases themselves either by trial and error, knowing a merchant who uses it, or having a friend or relative who works in the credit card center. Depending on the level of entry they have, they can do different things once inside the data unit.

A few years ago a number of people were arrested at a major credit card company who were offering to upgrade credit records to anything desired for $100. In other words, they would give you a $50,000 credit line for a mere $100 investment.

This went on for a number of months and involved up to ten employees before it was subsequently discovered and shut down. Not all the people who had their credit records updated, altered or erased were ever traced. This operation requires a higher level of entry than most hackers have at their finger tips as it requires an ever changing password that enables one to actually alter credit records. However, the simple entry password not changed very often, is fairly available.

A hacker or any one else with a telephone modem and a computer simply calls the credit agency or the credit card data base unit and gets the numbers, names, and

157

access and expiration dates of credit cards. He then uses them himself to order merchandise in any of the ways we've discussed or sells them to a more enterprising person or simply has someone else order it for him, splitting the merchandise between themselves.

This system is becoming more and more common and yet, at the same time, the countermeasures are obvious; encryption of data, changing of passwords and better computer security. One must remember, every time a password is changed, all the users on the system must be made aware of the new password, which entails a fair bit of hassle and expense on the part of the issuing company, so most passwords tend to be lazy and stay in service longer than they should.

MERCHANT ASSISTED THEFT

BLANK CARDS

It's far easier and cheaper for a would be credit card counterfeiter to simply take some white plastic sheets and emboss them using one of the techniques we've discussed. This can be accomplished either with an embossing machine or a use of hand embossing dyes or stamps.

Instead of going through the problems associated with copying, photo engraving, silk screening and/or printing, a section is cut out of white plastic approximately the size and shape of the credit card in question.

With the cooperation of a clerk or a small store owner, the merchandise can be purchased and this white card run through the embossing machine to leave the correct receipt.

The merchant realizes there is nothing on the card, no magnetic strip, it cannot be run through the electronic verifier nor can the credit center be consulted. This cannot be proven in follow up investigations as it will appear the numbers came off a real card or at least it will appear the embossing was close enough that the rest of the card probably appeared correct, thereby sliding the blame away from the merchant or the clerk.

After a certain number of bogus transactions there is going to be an investigation of the merchant. Something will be done to ascertain what is happening and someone involved will be caught.

The other possibility is that the bank will close the merchant's account (which they can legally do) and refuse to do business with them. Banks do talk to each other with regard to bad credit risks and fraudulent merchants. It then becomes difficult to open another account in the same name at any bank.

DOUBLE BILLING

To quote Gracie Slick, "He said hold a dollar bill up to a mirror and I'll show you something funny. It's only a fast buck but, oh, it's so hard to make that kind of money."

A very common transaction scam is for a retailer or clerk to run the same billing transaction through his credit card printer at least two times and then deposit both slips in his account. This provides a sort of instant loan which can improve his cash flow considerably at 0% interest.

If the credit card holder and/or bank does not catch the error, which is extremely likely since 80% of the credit card holders do not compare the receipts with billing statements, it's free money.

If the merchant is caught at it he simply blames a clerk, a computer error or whatever and issues credit for the over charges. This has still created a considerable amount of interest free money for several months for the merchant.

An interesting trick.

DOUBLE BILLING VARIATION

In this instance a clerk or cashier of a store or restaurant runs a slip through the card imprinter more than one time and then on the next cash transaction pockets the cash and enters the duplicate slip as though this new transaction was a legit transaction.

Over 80% of the people will not catch the error as they don't compare. Even if they do it is hard to trace down who did what by the time the credit card billing record comes through months later.

A slightly more complicated way of doing the same crime, albeit a safer method is for the clerk or cashier of the store or restaurant to take the duplicate slips and send them to an accomplice in another town who then submits the card receipts there where he works while mailing back his duplicates to his friend, thoroughly confusing the system while going past the three month limit for cross references and fairly effectively covering up any paper trail.

There is very little security for this except for merchants to watch very carefully the numbering of the credit card receipt book and demand to see any slips that are not filed.

SELF CREDIT

It is extremely easy for a clerk or employee of any merchant or mail order company to issue a fake charge back request to his own or to a friend's credit charge account. If he spreads it out right he will credit a number of high ticket refunds to the credit card number of friends who will split the money with him later. The cross referencing in these systems is very bad and the bank will assume the charge back is valid until the merchant prooves it otherwise.

Again, countermeasures are fairly difficult except for the merchant who keeps very good control of his credit card slips and makes sure unjustified charge backs do not occur and that every charge back is investigated. Most merchants will not bother to do this.

BANK CHEATS

It is possible for an employee who works for a bank or other credit card issuing institution or even a computer hacker to set up fake credit card accounts using new or unassigned credit card numbers in phony names. Then he can charge against the account, ordering merchandise and having it sent to friends, accomplices or to a mail drop. There's little fear of apprehension at this point as the information will be verified by the issuing company since they set up the account.

This can go on for some time and is extremely difficult to prove afterwards. The bank will not accept responsibility in most cases and will force the merchants to pay.

THE HAND IS QUICKER THAN THE EYE

Another extremely common trick for a merchant or store employee, especially a waiter or gas station attendant, is to collect expired cards or altered cards and accidentally return one of these cards, back to a legitimate customer in place of his own card. Most customers will not check the name on the card if it's the same type of card but just file it away in their wallet. This will go unnoticed until the next charge or may even slip past that giving the clerk or merchant a free and clear credit card. There's very little proof later as to where the switch may have occurred.

UNFULFILLED ORDERS

By far the simpliest way for any merchant to cheat credit card users is to take the orders, deposit the money and never ship the merchandise. By the time the unsatisfied customers write the postal inspectors (after a six week legal period) it will take a number of weeks or months for the postal inspectors to withhold mail and begin investigating the company. By this time the fraudulent company or merchant can have run up a substantial deposit. He then disappears, files bankruptcy, or shuts down.

THE DISAPPEARING MERCHANT

It's possible for any mail order or even retail establishment to offer an exceptional deal on a product, collect a number of credit card orders, run them through the bank, drain the account and disappear. Normally this will be done when the merchant is using a mail drop and will leave no paper trail behind to follow.

This sort of thing gives mail order a bad name.

A slightly different approach is for the merchant to get the credit card money and then spend it on equipment or services from which he receives kick backs. It can go to other companies he owns under different names that disappear or file bankruptcy. If it's a corporation that dies, there is no stigma attached to the actual owner when the corporation goes bankrupt and the assets are grabbed and sold off, but most phony companies will have zero assets anyway by this stage.

This transaction can be further complicated if the merchant establishes phony credit with other companies he owns or knows and places large, enticing ads for cheap merchandise to generate credit card orders and then even skips on paying the ads. In this case the merchant himself has virtually zero money invested and used fake ID to open the bank account, is long gone with a large chunk of cash before any investigation is launched.

167

MORE SELFISHNESS

Mail order and other retail marketing institutions themselves, many of whom measure their income in millions of dollars a year, (you can name many of them right off the bat) that sell similar products in similar catalogs to similar mailing lists, do not share bad risk names with each other. It would be a moderately simple matter in today's computerized industry and well worth the time and money to list bad names, bad numbers or bad addresses or even bad zip code areas and pass them among each individual mail order company in the same or similar business. This would eliminate charge backs of people who claim they didn't receive or order things on an habitual basis.

This would help eliminate the use of altered or counterfeit cards and generally would save marketers a lot of money. They do no do this. This makes it easy for a thief to go from one company to another to another with the exact same techniques, ordering the exact same merchandise.

168

DO IT YOURSELF

One of the least attempted and, when done well, most successful credit card crimes is the production of a counterfeit credit card. One that's good enough to pass as a real credit card without the help of a friendly merchant. A card that can be used almost anywhere for almost anything.

This may seem like a herculean task, but actually it has been done a number of times successfully and will go on being done until technology finds a way to finally identify the holder of every card, much like finger- prints or brain waves.

We interviewed a person, who shall remain nameless, who ran one of the largest successful credit card rings in the country for some time. This is his story. As usual, this is printed for informational purposes only. We do NOT advise you try this and if you are even thinking of doing anything like this, please, please, read the law that shows how you could indeed go to prison for many years.

On to the story.

Our counterfeiter, or as he prefers to call himself, entrepreneur, listed the things necessary to make a successful credit card from scratch. These include a printer or offset printing press (one might add that in the case of a printer, "dishonest" should be the adjective directly before "printer" as it is going to be dead obvious what you are doing). However, in today's world it is also easy to buy quite cheap offset printing presses that will do an adequate job of printing. Next one needs sheets of PVC white plastic (this is also easy to get) one white sheet for every run of cards plus one clear or frosted sheet for each run.

Special ink is also required. This must be a fast-drying ink, not a powder ink, that will dry on plastic when heated. Most inks are designed to dry only on paper which is porous and absorbs a certain amount of the ink, allowing the ink to dry. There are special inks created to dry without cracking or bubbling or smearing on non-porous surfaces such as PVC plastic . This ink must be employed in this production.

One also needs a heated electric hydraulic laminating machine. These are available simply by looking up companies that sell them and buying one. We're looking at a $3,000 investment here. The legit customer for such a machine is for a school, institution or large company (you won't be questioned too closely according to our friend because the machines do have legitimate uses). What they do is apply heat and pressure to laminate certain types of plastic together.

One also needs a special adhesive. This is available from Hughes Aircraft Company among other places. It must be an adhesive that is water-like and can be sprayed as a mist, but dries extremely clear under heat and will bond with ink. This is important. If it does not bond with ink (most glues will not) it will smear the ink or become loose where the ink rests. It may require some experimentation to find the correct type of glue and ink. It's part of the game. . .

One needs a camera to shoot the plates for the printing press or access to a printer with a camera.

THE PROCESS

If you've never looked at a credit card closely, take one and use a razor blade to split it apart down the edge. You'll notice it is made up of three layers of material. One is a colored and embossed layer of PVC plastic; two are clear or slightly frosted layers of plastic. These layers of plastic have been hydraulically bonded to each other and the clear layers prevent the ink from smearing on the embossed printed layer in the middle.

It is with this same three layer process that our friend made his cards. It's really the only way to go. Anything less is subject to suspicion and amateur enough to be noticed by even the most oblivious clerks.

To begin the process, one takes a sample credit card of the type being counterfeited and shoots it with a printer's camera, making an exact duplicate, sans name and numbers, of course, of the card.

This is a normal printing procedure and easy to do. Then this is made into a metal plate. It is always preferable to use metal instead of plastic plates as plastic just doesn't carry the same detail. Once the credit card has been shot onto a plate, it is loaded onto an offset press and sheets of PVC vinyl plastic are run through the press instead of paper. In other words, the ink is printed directly on the plastic itself. In the case of a two or four color credit card, it will take two to four runs through the press changing the color of the ink on each run to make a workable copy. This is just normal printing procedure and we are not going to go into any great detail here. Any printer knows how to do this.

The problem with the plastic is that it takes some special drying techniques when inked. The ink must be air dried. When the plastic is run through the off set press, heated air must be blown between the sheets keeping them separated, allowing the ink to dry. In some printing processes, a certain powder is used to keep the plates separate and dry the ink. This will not work for our process. The sheets must be held apart by heated air or they will stick together and smear the ink. Again - do not use drying powder at this stage.

Each sheet of vinyl plastic usually has four or more cards printed on it. It is run through the printer one side and then turned over. The second side is run through, depositing the necessary colors of ink, and printing both sides of the plastic. One now has a piece of plastic resembling a credit card but with no numbers, names, magnetic strip or signature area on it. In other aspects the cards will appear as real as a normal Visa,

Mastercharge or American Express credit card.

At this stage it is necessary to take the dried sheets of cards and apply the magnetic strip you see on the back of a real card. In reality this is a strip of magnetic material much like audio or video tape that contains pulses that are imprinted with the credit card number and the expiration date. That's all it is.

Most people, if they are using a manual imprinter for purchasing, never know what's on this tape, but it's necessary that the tape at least be in place.

If the credit card is run through a machine which verifies the tape or feeds it directly to a credit card company, it will reject the card.

It is very easy to erase these pulses on a legitimate credit card by sandwiching too many cards together in a wallet or keeping a magnetic lock door type card in with your credit cards. This proximity will wipe out the magnetic pulses on your cards. This goes for ATM cards, credit cards, door locks, etc., so it's not an instant bust to find a credit card with nothing on the strip.

However, the strip itself must be on the card. How is this done? If you will examine most credit cards, you'll find that a strip of VHS tape, taken from a VHS video cassette is exactly the same width and looks just like the magnetic tape strip on a credit card. The simplest thing to do at this stage is cut a piece of VHS tape to the correct length and lay it exactly on the spot on the credit card where the magnetic strip would normally go.

Once the above tape is applied, one is ready to laminate the card. This is done by taking our special adhesive and spraying it on both sides of the card sheet as a fine mist. Remember, this is a clear glue that dries without smearing the ink. As soon as this is done, the printed PVC sheet is placed very carefully between two sheets of clear plastic, one on either side. The adhesive will help hold it in place at this point.

Now the entire credit card sandwich sheet can go through the heated hydraulic press using two to four tons of pressure. Normally it will take five to six minutes with heat to laminate this clear plastic on both sides of the credit card, sealing the ink and the magnetic strip onto the card permanently. Some experimentation may be necessary with the temperature as plastics melt at different temperatures. Don't expect the first try to be the final try.

Once the five or six minutes have elapsed, the sheet must be allowed to cool, still under pressure in the machine, until it reaches about 90 degrees. Our friend also explained that one should use a stainless hydraulic press. This prevents the ink from smearing and does various things to the plastic that are not available with a lesser press. Not of course, that you are going to attempt this, but that's how he did it. Used a stainless steel press.

After it has cooled to about 90 degrees, the sandwich sheet can be removed from the press and the individual cards are cut out. A real pro will have a die made up to punch the cards out, making each one the correct size and rounding the corners correctly. If someone doesn't want to go to this expense one uses a round corner cutter (purchased at a regular stationery store) and cuts the single cards out making sure to round the corners as with a normal card.

At this point my friend had a number of blank credit cards, laminated on both sides with the correct ink and a magnetic strip. There was still no wording on the cards and no signature strip.

The signature strip problem can be solved in a couple ways. The easiest, quickest and often most effective way, is to take a strip of white adhesive bandage from the medicine cabinet and stick it on. This duplicates the signature strip of most cards quite effectively. It does not have the small printing that some modern cards have that says Visa or MasterCard nor are there little blue lines on it. It is possible to print up an adhesive paper strip with these correct words and use it as the signature strip. Most pros silk screen the signature strip onto the card. This is almost how it is done in real life. A good silk screen kit will put this white strip on the card very effectively allowing for the application of the signature as in a real credit card.

Then our nameless friend went out and looked up plastic card imprinters in the yellow pages under "plastic card imprinters". There are a number of machines manufactured to emboss and imprint on thin PVC plastic. Think of this as a hand held labeler. All it's doing is pressing up through the plastic to make letters and numbers. Most credit cards have two sizes of type and numbers on them and that's all. Most machines will do two sizes, however, you must make certain in advance. These machines can be purchased without embarrassing questions. They are used by schools, and hospitals to make ID cards, by senior citizens' homes, by clubs, or by membership stores. Manufacturing anything that requires raised or embossed lettering requires one of these printers.

They run about $1,000 and one simply dials or punches in the letter or number required and the machine then presses it into the plastic. There are some cheap Italian machines on the market, according to our nameless friend, that do not work well because their letters are of a different style than normal American credit card accepted lettering. In fact, our friend stuck in a plug for Addressograph Multilith as being the best machine on the market. Again, this is for informational purposes only.

It's also interesting to note that on a Visa card the V is not a typical V but is a slanted V. Most people will never notice this, but it is wise to be aware of it because most machines will not duplicate this slanted V.

Nor will the machine put different colored ink on top of the letters. Many modern credit cards use colored ink on top of the letters. As my friend explained, there are a couple ways to go about this. Most clerks do not notice that the ink is wearing or worn off the letters. The ink can be applied by taking the finished card with raised lettering and carefully pressing it on to a pad of the correct color ink. If this is done with just the right amount of pressure, only the raised letters will pick up the ink on the tips of the letters, as with a real credit card. Then a fixer can be sprayed on the card to help the ink remain on. The alternative is to take a roller and do the same thing. A smooth roller should apply ink only to the raised surfaces of the card allowing the remainder of the card to retain its original color.

The other option is to carefully take the die used in the imprinter machine and coat the inside of it with the correct color of ink so when it pushes the plastic through to form the letter, it will lay a layer of ink onto the letter or number. This is more difficult than it sounds. Experimentation on some machines will make it work.

Once a card has been imprinted and/or inked, one has for all intents and purposes, a plastic credit card with a number, (hopefully corresponding to a real number or at least corresponding to a bank number) a signature strip and a magnetic strip just like a regular credit card. This card will work for almost all purchases except those where a more modern merchant uses a verification device which reads the magnetic strip. You've seen these. They send it down the line directly to a central computer that verifies if the credit card is good.

Magnetic readers are available on the open market. In fact, for under $500 one can buy a magnetic strip reader for credit cards that hooks up to a computer with a serial port - IBM, Apple, etc. This will read the number on any credit card. If one wants to spend some money, for about $5,000 it is possible to buy a magnetic coder that will actually encode the VHS strip on the back of the card with any numbers one chooses to put on the card. In this way it is theoretically possible to make a credit card, complete with signature, numbers, lettering and encoded magnetic strip that will pass the most minute inspection by humans or by machine.

Yes, this is a lot of hassle. Yes, we're talking about an investment of thousands of dollars, a lot of patience, a lot of time, and a very dishonest attitude. However the rewards that can be gathered by a ring operating in this manner are high enough to make this a viable threat.

Anyone on both sides of the credit card fence, merchants or crooks, both should realize it is possible. Use the guidelines we dictate in this book to catch fraudulent cards, but a card that is made perfectly is as good as the real thing. In fact, it is the real thing.

SHORT CUTS

Besides the process we've just detailed, there are a couple of short cut methods often used by credit card counterfeiters. First, one takes a real card, a stolen card, or an expired card and shaves off the numbers and name. This gives a blank card that is coded and actually made by a credit card company. It only needs to be run through the embossing imprinter in order to put a new set of numbers and name on it.

This shaving has to be done very carefully so as not to leave traces that are pretty hard to miss.

If done correctly, this process provides a brand new card without going through any of the actual manufacturing or worrying about plastics, glues and other exotic problems.

Occasionally people attempt to iron a card. This is accomplished with a small heat source such as a soldering iron, wood burning gun or even a plain clothes pressing iron. The card is ironed flat.

If done correctly and if the heat is applied only to the areas where the numbers or letters are raised and not to the inked areas, this can actually melt the plastic back into a flat sheet which again can be re-imprinted with the credit card imprinter to give a brand new card.

There's one other method that bears mentioning. Although it sounds silly, more of this goes on than meets the eye. Take a piece of white plastic, buy the $1,000 imprinter and imprint the number and name on the plastic.

Obviously, this is not going to fool anyone, but if a person goes in cahoots with a merchant or someone who handles a large number of credit card transactions, this "card" can be run through the imprinter and will produce the same imprinting record as would a real credit card without the fancy colors, the inking and printing required or magnetic strip required by an actual credit card.

A large amount of bogus transactions can be run up, a large amount of merchandise can be sold under the counter or charges can be incurred with a simple piece of plastic and a machine purchased through the yellow pages.

It should be remembered that in any of the above methods, whether starting from scratch or altering a card the idea is to use real numbers. Numbers that have been gathered through any of a number of methods from stealing carbons, to paying off a cashier or finding someone who works in a bank to give you numbers, so you are actually using real numbers that will verify.

As means as this sounds, it should be pointed out that the owner of the numbers is not responsible for any payments.

COUNTERFEITING GOES INTERNATIONAL

Reports have recently come in from a number of Asian countries, including Thailand, Hongkong and even Japan of people counterfeiting American credit cards. These credit cards are usually American Express, Visa or MasterCards. They are produced with good manufacturing techniques.

In some cases, they are produced by manufacturing firms themselves and shipped into the United States in bulk where they are sold at $50 to $75 each. Professional rings order merchandise and resell with the hot cards.

These cards are quite well made and in most cases are passed without incident. The cards are becoming easier to get all the time. There have been a few arrests of students in the United States who were using these foreign forged cards to further their college careers.

Most of the cards that have been confiscated so far have had real numbers and names embossed on to them with the magnetic strip imprinted. Obviously, someone is getting credit card numbers and names from the United States, shipping them overseas where the cards are made up immediately and then shipped back into the country. This is probably just the tip of the iceberg and we'll see more and more of this as credit card use increases.

FLAT PLASTIC

Another interesting method of credit card alteration is to simply take the credit card and, using a hot iron, flatten out the numbers on a real credit card. It takes a little practice and the thief should have access to a card receipt machine that makes a copy to check the progress. When the numbers are flattened down just right, they'll still be legible upon a cursory visual inspection, however, when they are run through the receipt machine, they will not protrude enough to make an actual impression upon the credit card receipt.

If a clerk is astute enough to check and notices this, there's no harm done. You didn't know it. You don't know what happened. The card must be wearing out. It's very difficult to prove fraud or intent in this method, and most clerks will not notice the impression is too light to be read back at the main office and will simply pass the receipt on. In this case, of course, it is not billed. There is no way of tracing the merchandise or correlating what was bought with the card as the numbers simply can't be read.

The way around this is to train clerks and public contact personnel to take the time to check the receipt physically and make sure it actually did come through. In any high traffic time such as Christmas shopping time when there are temporary clerks working or when a store is busy because of a sale, people just don't have the time or inclination to actually check for this type of alteration.

COUNTERFEIT AND ALTERED CARDS: COUNTERMEASURES

It is possible to purchase or produce a viable counterfeit credit card. This is a credit card that is completely made up and not based on a real card. Since we've detailed the manufacture of these cards, let's look now at some countermeasures.

In the first place, a clerk can become familiar with the appearance of all major credit cards and simply look at each card for any abnormal signs or crude manufacturing - lamination separating, that would indicate a possible counterfeit. One of the first places to check is to see if the corners are square or rounded. Credit cards have rounded corners. If they look rough, if the signature tape doesn't look right, or the mag tape is on crooked, it can indicate a counterfeit.

It's possible for a retailer to check any card against the BIN (Bank Identification Number Directory) to see if the issuing bank does in fact exist and if the attempted purchaser knows the bank's name and address. On the other hand if one goes to the trouble of making good counterfeit credit cards, it is advisable to spend $1,000 and buy a BIN directory so the cards do verify to that extent.

It is also possible to purchase a rather expensive counterfeit detection machine, but very few retailers have this device on the premises. It's also possible to run the credit card through one of the electronic auto-dial information services. A crook will watch to see what the floor limit is or if the cards are being run through a verification process before attempting to use a counterfeit card.

Altered cards are much the same. Clerks should look for any sign of the signature being altered or removed. These strips are prepared so to effect major damage if erasure is attempted.   Many of the more modern Visa and Mastercharge have the word "Visa" or "Mastercharge" written in very small letters across the strip in ink that will erase easily. If any alteration is attempted, it is fairly obvious even to an untrained observer.

Secondly, a clerk should look for altered cards by checking if someone has painted on a black line where the magnetic strip should be. One should look closely at the numbers and make sure they are correct and appear to be evenly spaced rather than hand punched. Check it against the light to see if anything looks like it's been shaved, cut, or if the card's been altered and pasted together.

These are fairly amateurish alterations and most pros would not attempt to pass such crude efforts. However, if you look around the next time you make a purchase, you will notice very few clerks take even the most basic steps to detect counterfeit or altered plastic.

VISA HOTLINE

As we go to print, Visa USA, Inc. has just opened a brand new twenty-four hour hotline for law enforcement officers. This hotline is for use by officers in all branches of law enforcement and is to be employed in any investigation involving Visa credit cards and/or account numbers. Any enforcement agency who calls the number can get immediate confirmation over the phone that a card has been reported lost, stolen or it is a counterfeit. They will also get a referral to the security contact at the institution that issued the card.

Effectively this will mean the elimination of the grace period between the time the card is stolen and appears on the printed hot list. It will also allow enforcement agencies to tell if a card is counterfeit or altered in any way immediately and possibly apprehend the user.

Note this toll free number is not for the use of the general public nor is it for merchants. Rather, it is strictly for the use of law enforcement.

This raises an interesting question. How are they going to know if someone is actually law enforcement when they call over the phone? If a person was to call up and say he was Sgt. so and so of the Sonoff Beach police department and I'd like a check on Visa such and such, it's probably going to be read back to him without further verification of his status. The only security involved in this line is the phone number is not available to the general public.

The advantages to the person on the wrong side of the program with this line are, of course, the ability to immediately ascertain if a card is safe to use or has been reported stolen. Any suspicious card, any card that has exceeded it's normal time limit of use, any card that numbers may not match the name, can immediately be verified by any would-be thief.

We are not advising you to do this or take advantage of this line unless you are a law enforcement officer, in which case the line is 800-FOR-VISA, or translated into phone numbers 800-367-8472.

CRIME DOESN'T PAY OR DOES IT?

This is a true story. As they say on TV, names have been changed to protect the innocent or in this case, the juvenile.

Last year a 17-year old boy was arrested when he applied for a credit card at Trans Union Bank. Trans Union accessed its special file of fraudulent addresses and social security numbers, relayed the information to the security department at the bank, and the boy was arrested when he showed up to collect the credit card.

When he told his story some interesting facts came to light. He had 32 credit cards and in combination with loans had taken out approximately $300,000 worth of merchandise and cash during the past six months. This included a new Corvette and a condominium for which the mortgage information and money was obtained fraudulently.

He was arrested on two specific charges. The first charge was dropped when the real person behind the credit card refused to sign the affidavit charging the boy with fraud (note: the original owner was only responsible for $50 and probably thought it wasn't worth his time), the second charge was dropped when the case did not reach the Grand Jury during the legal time limit. The boy was not prosecuted and kept the merchandise. He is still driving the Corvette.

How did he do it? He started off when he was 16 by following the instructions laid out on the TV show 20-20. He applied for cards in his own name, altering the birthdate on the application forms and filling out a phony employment report stating he had worked for six years and gave a previous employer for four years. For employment phone numbers he would put down his father's phone number and he would answer the phone himself when the people called during the day toverify his employment.

At other times when applying for personal loans, he went to instant printers and had letterheads made up from employers verifying his employment and his salary. This was accepted at a number of banks in lieu of a W2 form when proof of employment was requested.

The boy took out a series of postal drop mail boxes, some of which required no ID or were very slack on their ID requirements and began to use these as home addresses. He then backed up his identification by buying phony ID's similar to the types still advertised in various magazines and by buying ID's and birth certificates on the street.

These ID's and birth certificates would be filled out using the real names of people. These names were gotten by going into businesses and picking up business cards and by running credit history reports on people who he got out of the phone book. Once he was armed with the information on the credit history report he made out the loan or credit card applications at one bank, then went into a branch bank utilizing the phony ID stated the loan had been approved and he would like a cashier's check.

In combination with using his father's name, his father's phone, his own name and a real driver's license which he obtained by phoning a letter from the school district stating he was of the correct age and applying for a driver's license, and using other people's names, he managed to get $300,000 worth of stereos, cars, cash, airline tickets and even a house.

One car salesman was so happy to have the sale consummated at the asking price that he helped phony up the papers knowing the boy was only 17 years old. They allowed the boy to sign his father's name to the required insurance proof form, even though that's illegal in the state of New York where all this transpired.

Sound too easy? Unfortunately it is all true and very easy to duplicate. Only a handful of people require notarization on loan applications and other forms and when the boy ran into this problem he simply had a notary seal made up from a supplier and notarized them himself. No one questioned it beyond this embossed proof.

To sum it up, using $8.00 illegally purchased ID's, phony birth certificates, and instant printers, $300,000 was lost from credit card issuing banks with no recourse and very little remorse.

DEBT COLLECTION

TECHNIQUES AND TRICKS OF MONEY COLLECTION

DEBT COLLECTION

The typical consumer may come in contact with three distinctly separate groups involved in money collection. The first group consists of retailers or lending institutions; i.e., department stores, mail order merchandise centers, utility companies or banks. The second group consists of collection agencies. The third final group would be attorneys.

Typically, the age of any debt determines which of the collection groups one will deal with. If you read your credit card statement you will notice there is a statement to the effect that this includes purchases on or before and gives a billing date. This date varies from company to company and determines when your debit is posted and becomes active (if you want to be clever, time your purchases for a day or two after your cut-off date and you'll automatically give yourself 25 days to one month "free" grace period).

Small businesses generally treat receivables or uncollected debts a bit more strenuously than do large businesses because of their cramped cash flow situation. Large corporations tend to show less enthusiasm in their debt collection policies.

Once your debt has reached the first day of the billing cycle, it becomes an outstanding asset a company wishes to collect. There are a couple rules of thumb companies follow in regards to collection attempts. The first is that the older a debt becomes, the more difficult it is to collect. The second is that when a debt is still young, the financial institution or store still considers you a valuable client and knows they have to be very careful as to not insult you and lose your business.

This attitude changes rapidly as the debt ages. Stores also realize people feel guilty when they owe money and if they are dunned too heavily will avoid doing further business with an institution because they feel as though a scarlet letter is sewn to the front of their jacket when they walk through the doors of a store that has sent them too heavy collection letters.

The first step to be taken to collect an overdue account is known as the reminder. A reminder may be printed on a customer's bill or may be sent out as a separate letter (usually a form letter as it costs time and money to collect a debt and most people will collect on the first reminder). Most reminders are issued within the first 30 days following the billing date. Sometimes they may be posted as soon as 10 days after bills are sent out. Other establishments may wait the full 30 days before sending out the first reminder.

Institutions realize that not everyone is financially viable 100% of the time and they assume an unpaid bill on an otherwise good credit record indicates a temporary money shortage or that the consumer lost the bill or possibly that the bill never arrived. A friendly reminder in the form of "did you forget us?" or other cute little saying is the first step employed.

After a debt becomes 60 days old, the issuing establishment is going to become more concerned. They still want to keep your business so form letters most probably will be sent out at a 10 day interval each one bearing slightly stronger language inquiring if there is some problem with the account or urging you to give the company a call to let them know what's going on.

At the end of 60 days one can expect a phone call from the company which will still be moderately polite but will inquire as to the problem in payment and how you plan on resolving it. Phone calls are a favorite form of debt collection because they are quick and do not cost too much in the way of time or revenue. They also tend to be a personal message that instills fear in the average consumer and encourages rapid payment.

If the debt is allowed to reach 90 days without payment one risks crossing over the fine line into consumer abandonment. If the institution has not made a phone call yet, they soon will.

At this point, the issuing institution will cancel your account and most likely refuse to issue you further credit. You will also be informed that your debt is about to be turned over to a collection agency or attorney and horrendous punishment on both you and your credit record are sure to follow. Some of this is true, some of it is not.

At the end of a three-month billing period, if no payment has been received the account may be turned over to a outside collection agency or if size (normally at least $1,000) warrants it, directly to an attorney.

The establishment has decided they do not wish to be associated with you. They are taking leave of you as a customer.

COLLECTION AGENCIES

A collection agency is a commission-operated business; they keep an average of 50% of each debt they collect. For this reason they are usually a last ditch effort as far as a retail merchant or bank is concerned.

Collection agencies do not work for consumers and are completely uninterested in maintaining any semblance of friendship or good will with consumers in general. They are concerned with collecting the money owed by whatever means, legally and sometimes otherwise, available to them. Collection agencies consider anyone who fall under their domain to be a flake or deadbeat and will show no mercy unless they feel it is in their interest to do so.

Because of the cost to the merchant of using a collection agency, in the past merchants have formed their own internal collection agencies with a separate name and letterhead. These shadow agencies are held as a threat to non-paying consumers. The Fair Debt Collection Act outlawed this shoddy process along with many other procedures used in the past by collection agencies.

In the past a number of collection agencies have run afoul of the law by using outrageous threats, harassment, anonymous phone calls, etc. in an attempt to collect debts. The Fair Debt Collection Act has at least curbed the most outrageous of these excesses.

In 1971 a man who was in charge of a standard collection agency in New York City was indicted on 45 counts of grand larceny, harrassment, and extortion for his efforts to collect overdue bills. A number of other agencies and people have been in trouble with the law for over zealous impulses.

Collection agencies know they will collect at best one-third of the debts they take on as these people are considered to be deadbeats or already written off by standard collection techniques and may also be a bit more hard boiled after dealing with the merchant's attempts to collect.

Typically collection agencies will begin with a number of letters demanding final payment, threatening to mess up your credit for the rest of your life, and other dark threats if payment is not forthcoming within the internal time period set up by each agency (much as with the original merchant) and they will begin calling you on the telephone and asking why the debt hasn't been paid and what you plan to do about it. There are very strict rules established as to what they can say over the phone, who they can call, and what they can do to collect this debt.

If the money is not forthcoming within a reasonable period of time, the collection agencies will usually threaten legal action. One should realize it is against the principles of good business to actually take legal action for debts under $1,000 and that's a minimum. Many agencies have a much higher ceiling and even sleazy attorneys will rarely operate on a contingency basis for any money less than this as they know they are likely to involve themselves in a procedure which will require output in both paperwork and time.

Most people simply do not play by ignoring the bill collectors although occasionally a person will take matters in hand threatening the agency back. Some try to delay the agency and others may wait until a number of dunning letters have been received and then offer to make a settlement with the agency.

Most agencies will accept any reasonable settlement since they know they may not get anything if this procedure is allowed to continue. If a creditor offers a settlement he should be certain the agency understands the terms of the settlement and will not harm his credit rating out of sheer malice. Many agencies will not harm a consumer's credit rating even if they threaten to over a bad debt because it costs them time and money to write letters to the various credit reporting agencies and report the debt. They realize they may have to verify the debt any number of times in the future which consumes more time.

In many small debts such as mail order or newspaper ads, they only have the name and possibly the phone number of the consumer to go by and do not have enough information to possibly enter any record of the bad debt with a credit reporting agency. They legally can report uncollected bad debts and some may do so because they want to set an example and are not happy with the consumer. This is especially true of larger debts.

In the section entitled, "Collection Agency Technique Guide" we have listed a number of the techniques collectors are taught to employ when dealing with potential bad creditors. These techniques are legal and are designed to extract maximum payment from any creditor.

One universal point to notice here is that collection agencies will rarely ever identify themselves over the phone. They will use a name, often a phony name, when trying to reach the consumer. This leads to messages such as, "Have John call Susan at 832-2222. It's very important." The main thing they are trying to do is get in touch with the consumer so they can start to make him feel guilty or demand payment.

A wise consumer screens his calls both at home and in his business by asking, "Who wants to know?" They say who and then one should ask what firm they are with before saying whether the person is in or not. Legally they have to identify themselves if asked to do so over the telephone.

If one wants to speak with someone at a collection agency, the first thing one should do is ask if this is their real name and not a business name supplied at the agency. Never be put on the defensive by a collection agency is a wise rule to live by.

We'll look at some legal no no's for a collection agency but first always remember that by law if you tell a collection agency you do not want to hear from them any more, they must stop contacting you. Be advised that at this point they will either drop the debt or proceed to the next stage which may include legal action, but they must stop contacting you per your request.

FAIR DEBT COLLECTION ACT - WHAT COLLECTION AGENCIES MAY NOT DO

Collection agencies or collectors may not contact anyone but your attorney with the exception they may ask other people where you live or work. They cannot discuss your debt or payment history with anyone else.

They cannot contact you at work if they are made aware that your employer disapproves of this practice. They may not call you at any inconvenient time or place. This is normally construed to mean any time before 8:00 a.m. or after 9:00 p.m., unless you ask them to do so.

They cannot force the consumer to incur any expense for talking to them. They cannot send you postage due mail or call collect. It is interesting to note American Express has a habit of calling from their internal collection agency in Florida leaving a message to call back the person at the agency long distance without stating that it is American Express calling. This is a fine line as you can call back and as such incur a phone bill. They do not accept collect calls.

They may not tell anyone else you owe money or advertise your debt in any way or publish a list of non-paying deadbeats.

They cannot threaten violence or harm to you or your property nor can they use profane language or behavior to "harass, oppress or abuse" anybody.

194

They cannot use the telephone to constantly annoy you and must identify themselves on every call if asked to do so.

They cannot threaten to take legal action unless they actually plan to do so.

They cannot continue attempting to reach the consumer if they are specifically asked to stop.

They cannot use a fictitious name in trying to collect a debt. In the past collection agencies have tried to pretend to be law firms or credit bureaus or even government agencies. This is not legal nor is any threat of arrest. Even if you go to court, it is civil court. This is not a criminal action in any sense of the word in this country.

They cannot contact you by post card because someone else could read the card.

They cannot put anything on the outside of an envelope that shows the letter is regarding an outstanding debt.

They are not allowed to give false information about you to anyone nor are they allowed to make false statements while trying to collect a debt.

They cannot deposit a post-dated check before the date on the check nor are they allowed to ask for a post-dated check.

Collectors conduct psychological warfare. They have heard all the excuses and are really not interested in the reasons for non-payment. They survive on their ability to extract blood from turnips.

Over zealous collectors may exceed the law in their efforts to collect monies due. They may not be aware of the law in all cases. If a consumer responds to a collection agency's phone call by asking for the real name of the collector, the name and address of the agency, the name of the collector's supervisor and states the facts, he is likely to find the agency switches to being defensive and will respect his rights to a much greater degree than they did before.

If you feel a collection agency has violated your rights in any way, contact the Federal Trade Commission and file a formal complaint within 30 days of the violation. It is also possible to file a civil law suit if there are grounds to do so within one year of any violation.

ATTORNEYS

There's an old saying, "if there's one attorney in town, he makes good money. If there's two, they get rich." From any viewpoint there's some truth in this saying. One way to look at the legal profession is that they exist to perpetuate their own existence. Lawyers can complicate simple matters to require other lawyers to get involved.

If your debt is substantial enough and a collection agency or even the merchant feels he has no chance of collecting, he may turn it over to an attorney. The attorney may file a lawsuit in order to get a judgment against you.

The first step in filing a lawsuit is to serve you with a summons. A summons may be served by a private server, a private person over 18 (in most states) or by a deputy sheriff. Most states require an attorney to try to serve a summons three times before what is known as substitute service.

If you are not found after three legitimate tries, most states allow a relative, boss or neighbor to be served and a duplicate summons mailed to you. If you do not show up in court after receiving a legitimate summons, you will lose the case by default. A default judgment stands as strong as actually losing the case.

In some instances, usually in economically depressed areas, summons servers may not try to serve the summons but instead dispose of it and sign a paper saying he did serve it. He is betting that the consumer will not challenge or have enough knowledge of his own rights to challenge the default judgment that will follow such an act.

If you show up in court you can produce an affirmative defense. You have an opportunity to tell your side of the story with an attorney. You may win the case or the judge may grant a partial judgment to the plaintiff.

Attorneys will often attempt to collect by using a strong letter or phone call before actually going to the trouble or expense of filing a lawsuit against you. They may point out if you lose the case, you are facing horrendous consequences including legal costs. Legal costs rarely amount to very much and are generally inconsequential considering the settlement of a large debt.

Smart attorneys will often run an asset and credit check on the consumer and if no assets appear they will not bother to go through the lawsuit as they generally work on a contingency basis.

If you lose the suit the attorney may now proceed to garnish your salary (or percentage of your salary) and he can legally seize most assets that you own. Many people who lose this type of lawsuit may have zero assets and no job or no job of record. If this happens the attorney will subpoena you to reappear in court and the judge will, under penalty of perjury, make you list your assets and ask you how you plan to pay the judgment. If you are unable to meet the requirements in the foreseeable future, it is possible the courts will force you into bankruptcy or suggest that you consider this road as you are legally responsible for the judgment.

If you are given terms by the court to discharge the debt and you fail to meet these terms, the court may charge you with contempt. It is possible you could be facing jail time.

Legal ways to avoid this situation includes bankruptcy and appearing in court to convince the judge you have no means at your disposal to pay off the debt.

If you leave town or disappear and the outstanding debit is large enough, the attorney will hire a skip tracer or even a private detective to track you down. For a detailed look at the methods involved on both sides of the skip tracing fence, I suggest you read, "How To Get Anything on Anybody", by Lee Lapin.

LEGAL COLLECTION TECHNIQUES

The following techniques have been compiled from guides available to insiders in the collection business. They cover most situations that might possibly arise and are designed to be used over the telephone.

The first collection call should be made at a convenient time and one should not annoy, press or harass the person reached but one should be forceful and tactful in asking about the debt.

Do not call the person at their employment if your state forbids this or if you have been notified their employer does not want to receive such calls.

Always identify yourself but do not give the name of your employer.

Once you are certain you have actually reached the consumer you may identify your employer and state the purpose of your call.

A good approach is to ask a deadbeat for his or her help. Tell them why you are calling and ask them if they could help you by paying XX amount of dollars, which normally is the full amount, at once because they are overdue.

Attempt to motivate the deadbeat by stressing the importance of his fulfilling his promise to pay.

Get a solid reason for non or late payments and then ask the consumer when his payday is, if he will mail or bring the check by at this time.

Always inquire as to the name of his bank, his account number, his employer, spouse's employer if viable, his address, his phone number, if there is any other number he can be reached at.

If you extract a promise always tell them you will confirm these arrangements by mail and then do so.

Provide reasons the deadbeat should pay his debt immediately. These include: to maintain a good credit record (convince him his credit record is one of his important assets in life, but do not threaten to report it to a credit reporting agency unless you intend to do so); reaffirm you know it is his intention to do the correct thing and he is honest and reliable and this is just a temporary situation that you know he wants to clear up; act very appreciative that he is paying now; stress he appreciated getting the credit in the first place and he can now free himself from worry, protect his credit rating, and generally re-establish his reputation by paying the debt now; bring up he'll avoid all additional costs that may be incurred if legal action is required (by law you must not state you intend to take such action unless you actually intend to do so); remind him further actions will give you no choice but to turn this account over to a collection agency or an attorney, but don't dwell on the specifications of such action, let the person fear the consequences without knowing exactly what they are.

If the deadbeat gives you a specific reason for non-payment such as illness, pin him down to the specifics of the situation. Is he ill? How long has he been off work? When does he plan to return to work? Where does he work? Ask for a time you can expect payment. If the deadbeat is nebulous on payment, emphasize he must stay in touch with you on specific times which you give him in order to arrange "continuation" of the grace period you are allowing him.

If the party claims to be divorced or separated and uses this as a reason for non-payment, obtain all specifics including the date of the dissolutionment or divorce, the name and phone number of both attorneys involved and advise him you still expect payment from him and you consider him responsible for the account. Always ask for

200

payment. If you get an attorney's name at this stage, contact the attorney directly to verify all information. If no payment is forthcoming, obtain a promise of continued contact on specific dates.

If the deadbeat claims bankruptcy, cease collection efforts because a court is now involved. Be certain to make no threats at this stage and operate only under the Fair Debt Collection Practices Act. Obtain the date of bankruptcy, the document number and the name of the attorney in involved and contact the attorney directly.

File a proof of claim and plan on attending a "first meeting" of the creditors with your attorney, depending on whether your attorney wants you there or not. Ask your attorney what questions you can ask the creditor and still remain legal. If it is a secured claim, know that the debtor may have the right to redeem certain secured merchandise by paying the creditor only the fair market value as determined by the bankruptcy court.

It is possible to convince the consumer to sign a new note. This must be approved by the bankruptcy court. Always be aware of possible fraud or of the filing of false financial statements involved in any bankruptcy.

If it is an unsecured claim, pry on the deadbeat's moral status. You know he wants to keep his reputation together and do the correct thing even though he is in economic straits. You'll be happy to arrange a payment schedule that fits his new status in order to help protect him.

If you are informed that the deadbeat died, take a sympathetic attitude while asking for the date and place of death as well as the name and address of the administrator of his estate and the probate number. Then file a creditor's claim and tactfully inquire if there is any life insurance, the amount, the beneficiaries, and ask for payment even if there is probate.

If you are informed the deadbeat is not at home or not available when you call, identify yourself but do not identify your employer unless you are specifically asked to do so. Never say the deadbeat owes money, if they ask why you are calling, state that you are correcting your address information file on the consumer. Always obtain as much information as possible from each phone contact including the telephone number and current address of the deadbeat, his employer, his spouse's employer and when he will be available to answer the phone. Leave your name and telephone number and stress the importance of a return call.

It is also possible to ask if it is o.k. to phone the deadbeat at his job thereby giving you permission to do so.

Be tactful but forceful and always ask for payment. If you can't extract a promise of payment, always establish a calendar for future contacts and remember the first 20 seconds after a phone is answered is the most important time of the call.

JUDGMENT PROOFING

Once an attorney or creditor obtains a judgment against a consumer he must still collect the amount owed. A smart attorney will check for your bank account, any car registered in your name, your wages and any real property you have registered.

Judgment proving is a method of limiting access to your assets through a number of legal and semi-legal means. In the first place there are federal exemptions from judgments which include benefits of the Veteran's Administration, federal disability funds, CIA retirement funds just in case you happen to be retired from the CIA, civil service retirement funds and social security trust funds, not to mention the infamous payments made to widows of employees of the U.S. Lighthouse Service.

Granted these are not likely to protect too much of your money but each state also has its own exemptions. You need to check with an attorney to find out exempt items in your state. Even if items are listed, these exemptions are not automatic. You have to claim your right to them in order to take the exemption. Generally things exempted under state rules are tools you need to conduct your business, household furnishings, the clothes on your back and any houses you have homesteaded.

Speaking of that, homesteading is a good idea if you feel you may be in financial hot water. Once you file the homestead paper with the state, you can homestead your house. This protects a certain percentage of the value of the house, which is established by your state. The papers must be filed correctly and usually require an attorney to do so.

Sometimes getting a divorce or separation can protect you from collection agencies and attorneys. Depending on where you reside, you may not be responsible for your past debts and if you transfer assets into your spouse's name, they won't be seized.

Sometimes it is possible to incorporate which may protect various assets. An attorney is required to do this correctly.

You can always take money out of your bank account but be advised if you take it out after a judgment, it is possible the court may see this as fraud and will require proof of the necessity of removing the money and where it went. It is better to take it out in advance.

If your wages are garnisheed you can sometimes prove that your wages barely cover the "necessities of life" and you need them to support yourself and your family. If the court sees this to be true the judge may exempt your wages from garnishment.

It is possible that state law may protect a certain amount of equity in a vehicle. If you check in advance of the judgment and discover your state protects a smaller equity than you have in the vehicle it may be wise to sell the vehicle and buy another one on time so you have little or no equity. Then the vehicle will not be seized to pay the judgment.

In some states it is possible to refinance your own car so you have no equity or sign the car over to a friend after he signs a note to pay you off in time. If the car is repossessed and you can prove lack of ownership or no equity the repossession company will have to return the car to you.

I

STALLING TRICKS

Even after a bill is received there are a number of tried and true tricks to put off payment until such a time that your cash flow may be in better shape. These tricks include: saying the check is in the mail (this excuse is actually on record as being used four days after formation of the pony express in the early 1800's. It still works today although wise collection agencies will inquire about the specifics of the payment such as the dollar amount, the account number, the time and date of mailing, etc.).

"Forgetting" to sign the check. Banks legally cannot cash a check that is not signed and if the creditor does not notice the lack of signature, it can be a month or longer for the check to be returned by his bank to him and him to you with a note asking you to correct your error.

Alternating the numbers on the check. If your check has magnetic numbers at the bottom, rubbing them against a large stereo speaker magnet will erase the number. If they are optically read they can be altered with a razor blade. Either method will kick the check back as a computer error or cause the bank to manually process it, sticking on a separate sticker with the account number and gaining you valuable time without seeming to incur any fault on your part.

Some people simply put the wrong check in with the wrong bill. You can put the power company's check in the telephone company's bill, the telephone company's check in the department store's bill. . . The credit department will normally return the check to you explaining you made an error and asking you to forward the check to them. It is possible to stall this out longer by calling and ascertaining they did not actually receive the check, saying you will have to put a stop payment on it and try to find it but will mail them another one in a couple days.

Stopping payment on a check. This does not incur the same wrath as when a check bounces, although you will get a call from the creditor inquiring about the reason for the stopped payment. A wise consumer usually expresses horror upon receipt of such a phone call blaming the error on his secretary or other non-involved personnel claiming he meant to stop a check from their dishonest competitor and ask them to mail the check back.

Bouncing the check. It is against the law to bounce checks, but the only time prosecution actually takes place is when intent can be proven. Innocent people bounce checks all the time, sometimes with good excuses and never go to jail. Habitual paper hangars, on the other hand, can be prosecuted. If an account is closed there is a implied legitimacy of the check not clearing and most creditors will accept a reasonable excuse if a promise of a new check is forthcoming.

Write a check for a specific amount, which is much less than the actual debt. Before this check clears, write a letter to the credit department telling them you are sorry but you made an error. You sent them too much money and please refund the $7 extra you included in the last check. Before they respond to this, write them another check for a small specific amount to cover the "adjusted balance". This is a method of confusing and tiring credit managers that will either a. irritate them beyond belief and motivate them to get on your case or b. get them tired of you to the point where they will accept the check and stamp "paid" on the account.

One can contact the creditor directly and ask for a grace period because of a temporary problem. Most creditors will welcome this type of contact and grant the request assuming you have been a good customer in the past and they want to keep your business.

BANKRUPTCY

The number of personal bankruptcies filed in the United States has been constantly on the rise for the past 20 years. The concept of bankruptcy is to allow the person who has made an error in his financial judgment to begin afresh with the proverbial clean slate under arm.

One may notice that banks and other financial institutions now post warnings advising consumers to avoid bankruptcy like the plague, regardless of their attorney's advice. The reasons behind such warnings are obvious. Creditors tend to lose far more in bankruptcy actions than do debtors.

The reality of bankruptcy is that it is sometimes a necessary step to pull one out of debts that one cannot otherwise clear while protecting certain assets. It will also stay on one's credit record for a minimum of 10 years and may inhibit the granting of further credit during that time. Any bankruptcy costs everybody money. Creditors stand to lose a major portion of their debts since by very definition, bankruptcy infers the debtor does not have the necessary assets to pay his debts in full.

It will also cost the consumer money in lawyer's fees and court costs. Any but the most inexperienced attorneys demand payment in bankruptcy proceedings upfront in cash.

Because of the realities of bankruptcy, it can be an effective tool to re-negotiate outstanding debts. If a letter to a creditor lists specific reasons the debts cannot be paid and suggests an alternate re-payment plan ending with such a plan is your only hope to avoid bankruptcy, many creditors will go along knowing their only alternative is to lose a major portion of the debt.

Certain debts are not covered by the bankruptcy statutes. These include:

Federal Income Tax and Income Tax Penalties

Debts Owed to the Government

Debts Not Listed in the Bankruptcy Petition

Alimony or Child Support

Any Debt Incurred by Fraudulent Means (this exemption will also apply to items on credit cards or lines of credit when the court believes the consumer had no intention of fulfilling the original debt)

There are two types of bankruptcies. The first is known as Chapter 7 or straight bankruptcy. Under Chapter 7 the court will declare you bankrupt if your debts far outweigh your assets. Most of your assets with the exception of judgment proofed or state and federal exemptions will be seized in order to pay off your debts. The debts are paid off in a specific order determined by the court and the bankruptcy will remain on your credit report for 10 years.

When your attorney files bankruptcy, all creditors are prohibited from making further efforts to collect debts. The court will send notices to all the creditors you list on your petition of bankruptcy and set up a meeting of the creditors. There is normally only one meeting and it is held in the bankruptcy court. You will be questioned about your assets and income and the court will decide what portion of your assets it will take and sell to discharge the debts to your creditors.

CHAPTER 13, THE WAGE EARNERS PLAN

Chapter 13 is an alternative to straight bankruptcy. Under this plan the consumer asks to set up an installment paying program through the court in lieu of having his assets confiscated and sold. The plan lasts for three years and can be extended for two more if circumstances so warrant.

During the pay-back period the consumer may not take on any new debts and must not fail to discharge the obligations he has set up. There are some exemptions to this and the court will take notice of special circumstances such as sickness or unemployment.

This plan is similar to the use of a credit counselor except a court appointed trustee will be in charge of the program.

If you successfully complete the Chapter 13 repayment program, the court may discharge the rest of your debts, even if they are not paid in full.

Chapter 13 stays on your record for seven years and credit institutions tend to treat it much as they would Chapter 7. You should realize your life style will not change for the better for at least three years and you will probably end up paying a lot more cash than you would if you file straight bankruptcy. It also requires the approval of all your secured creditors and most of your unsecured creditors. This approval is not as difficult to obtain as one might suspect as creditors realize they will get more from you under the Chapter 13 guidelines than they would if you file Chapter 7. Most people who reach this stage will file Chapter 7 if the Chapter 13 plan is not approved.

It is generally a good idea to negotiate with your creditors to set up your own payment plan or seek the help of a professional credit counselor who will do (for a fee) this negotiation for you. This type of negotiation will cost you less than filing for Chapter 13, assuming you have no lawyer's or court fees and will not put the stain of a bankruptcy on your credit record.

If such negotiations fail completely, Chapter 13 is often a viable alternative.

In either type of bankruptcy the services of a lawyer are strongly recommended, even though blank forms can be purchased through book stores. An attorney's help in this case is worth every cent.

LAWS AND LETTERS

CREDIT ACTS AND DISPUTE LETTER SAMPLES

A

SETTLEMENT SAMPLE

John Doe
1313 Lucky Ave.
Easy Street, CA 94403

Mr. Dragon
XXXCompany
1414 Sleazy St.
San Francisco, CA 94074

Dear Mr. Dragon:

As a result of an accident my situation has suffered due to unemployment and I find I can't pay my debt to your firm. My lack of income leaves nothing for such payments. It is impossible for me to raise cash to satisfy you or other creditors since I have no real property to sell.

I can, however, offer you a settlement of 30 cents on the dollar as payment in full for this obligation. Since my balance with your firm is $1,800, I am willing to send you $600 as payment in full next Monday, after I cash my last paycheck.

If you are willing to accept this offer, please sign and return this letter to me as soon as convenient.

Respectfully yours,

John Doe

Accepted by:

_____ _____
                          Date

B

CREDIT REPORT LETTER

March 11, 1989

Biller Credit
4818 Sleazy St.
Detroit, MI 48018

ATTN: CUSTOMER RELATIONS DEPARTMENT

Dear Sir:

Please mail me a copy of my current credit report.

John Doe   Susan Ann Doe
1414 Easy St.
San Francisco, CA 94403

Previous address includes:
8181 Rough St.
Mill Valley, CA 94407

Soc. Security No: Spouse Soc. Sec. No.:

Credit Denied By: (if denied within previous 30 days)

Check for $10 enclosed.

Respectfully yours,

John Doe

C

DISPUTE LETTER

John Doe
1414 Easy St.
San Francisco, CA 94403
Soc. Sec. #
Date of Birth

Date

Biller Credit
4818 Sleazy St.
Detroit, MI 48018

Dear Sirs:

I formally request that the following items be immediately investigated. I would like them removed in order to show my true credit history as these items should not be on my account. They are injurious to my credit history since they are inaccurate.

Subscriber Name: Swing City
Subscriber #:
Account #:

I would also like to point out that the following credit inquiries were never authorized by me:

Subscriber Name: Great Used Cars
Subscriber #:
Date of Inquiry:

Please complete your new investigation and send me my updated credit report.

Thank you for your time and consideration.

Respectfully,

John Doe

D

DISPUTE LETTER
(For Items Inaccurately Reported in Credit Reports)

John Doe
1313 Lucky Ave.
Easy Street, CA 94403
Soc. Sec. #:
Date of Birth

Biller Credit
4818 Sleazy St.   Date
Detroit, MI 48018

Sirs:

Even after an investigation, the items I have listed below should not appear on my
credit report. They are not true and are highly injurious to my credit rating.

Subscriber Name: Upchuck Appliances
Subscriber #:
Account #:

Please re-investiage this claim. Kindly submit the names and addresses of each
person with whom you verified this information to me as stipulated in "The Fair Credit
Reporting Act," Public Law 91-508 Titlve VI, Section 611, Subsection A-D.

Please send a copy of your new report after the new credit investigation.

Thank you for your time and consideration.

Respectfully,

John Doe

E

DISPUTE LETTER

John Doe
1313 Lucky St.
Easy Street, CA 94403
Soc. Sec. #:
Date of Birth:

Date:

Biller Credit
4818 Sleazy St.
Detroit, MI 48018

Dear Sirs:

On March 11, 1989 I wrote asking you to investigate several items on my credit report.

I have not received any response from you. You are required to respond within a "reasonable period of time" under the Fair Credit Reporting Act. I believe that time is at hand.

Respectfully,

John Doe

THE FAIR CREDIT REPORTING ACT PUBLIC LAW

The Fair Credit Reporting Act became effective on April 25, 1971. The Fair Credit Reporting Act (Public Law 91-508), sets certain guidelines credit bureaus and creditors must follow in reporting a consumer's credit file, as well as giving the consumer certain rights as discussed in this section. Enclosed is a copy. It is imperative you **read it.**

TITLE VI-PROVISIONS RELATING TO CREDIT REPORTING AGENCIES

Amendment of Consumer Credit Protection Act

Sec. 601. The Consumer Credit Protection Act is amended by adding at the end thereof the following new title:

"TITLE VI-CONSUMER CREDIT REPORTING

"Sec. 601. Short title
"This title may be cited as the Fair Credit Reporting Act.

"Sec. 602. Findings and purpose
"(a) The Congress makes the following findings:

"(1) The banking system is dependent upon fair and accurate credit reporting. Inaccurate credit reports directly impair the efficiency of the banking system, and unfair credit reporting methods undermine the public confidence which is essential to the continued functioning of the banking system.

"(2) An elaborate mechanism has been developed for investigating and evaluating the credit worthiness, credit standing, credit capacity, character, and general reputation of consumers.

"(3) Consumer reporting agencies have assumed a vital role in assembling and evaluating consumer credit and other information on consumers.

"(4) There is a need to insure that consumer reporting agencies exercise their grave responsibilities with fairness, impartiality and a respect for the consumer's right to privacy.

"(b) It is the purpose of this title to require that consumer reporting agencies adopt reasonable procedures for meeting the needs of commerce for consumer credit, personnel, insurance, and other information in a manner which is fair and equitable to the consumer, with regard to the confidentially, accuracy, relevancy, and proper utilization of such information in accordance with the requirements of this title.

"Sec. 603. Definitions and rules of construction
"(a) Definitions and rules of construction set forth in this section are applicable for the purposes of this title.

"(b) The term 'person' means any individual, partnership, corporation, trust, estate, cooperative, association, government or governmental subdivision or agency, or other entity.

"(c) The term 'consumer' means an individual.

"(c) The term 'consumer' means an individual.

"(d) The term 'consumer report' means any written, oral, or other communication of any information by a consumer reporting agency bearing on a consumer's credit worthiness, credit standing, credit capacity, character, general reputation, personal characteristics, or mode of living which is used or expected to be used or collected in whole or in part for the purpose of serving as a factor in establishing the consumer's eligibility for (1) credit or insurance to be used primarily for personal, family, or household purposes, or (2) employment purposes, or (3) other purposes authorized under section 604. The term does not include (A) any report containing information solely as to transactions or experiences between the consumer and the person making the report; (B) any authorization or approval of a specific extension of credit directly or indirectly by the issuer of a credit card of similar device; or (C) any report in which a person who has been requested by a third party to make a specific extension of credit directly or indirectly to a consumer conveys his decision with respect to such request, if the third party advises the consumer of the name and address of the person to whom the request was made and such person makes the disclosures to the consumer required under section 615.

"(e) The term 'investigative consumer report' means a consumer report or portion thereof in which information on a consumer's character, general reputation, personal characteristics, or mode of living is obtained through personal interviews with neighbors, friends, or associates of the consumer reported on or with others with whom he is acquainted or who may have knowledge concerning any such items of information. However, such information shall not include specific factual information on a consumer's credit record obtained directly from a creditor of the consumer or from a consumer reporting agency when such information was obtained directly from a creditor of the consumer or from the consumer.

"(f) The term 'consumer reporting agency' means any person which, for monetary fees, dues, or on a cooperative nonprofit basis, regularly engages in whole or in part in the practice of assembling or evaluating consumer credit information or other information on consumers for the purpose of furnishing consumer reports to third parties, and which uses any means or facility of interstate commerce for the purpose of preparing or furnishing consumer reports.

"(g) The term 'file' when used in connection with information on any consumer, means all of the information on that consumer recorded and retained by a consumer reporting agency regardless of how the information is stored.

"(h) The term 'employment purposes' when used in connection with a consumer report means a report used for the purpose of evaluating a consumer for employment, promotion, reassignment or retention as an employee.

"(i) The term 'medical information' means information or records obtained, with the consent of the individual to whom it relates, from licensed physicians or medical practitioners, hospitals, clinics, or other medical or medically related facilities.

"Sec. 604. Permissible purposes of reports

"A consumer reporting agency may furnish a consumer report under the following circumstances and no other:

"(1) In response to the order of a court having jurisdiction to issue such an order.

"(2) In accordance with the written instructions of the consumer to whom it relates.

"(3) To a person which it has reason to believe--

"(A) intends to use the information in connection with a credit transaction involving the consumer on whom the information is to be furnished and involving the extension of credit to, or review or collection of an account of, the consumer; or

"(B) intends to use the information for employment purposes; or

"(C) intends to use the information in connection with the underwriting of insurance involving the consumer; or

"(D) intends to use the information in connection with a determination of the consumer's eligibility for a license or other benefit granted by a governmental instrumentality required by law to consider an applicant's financial responsibility or status; or

"(E) otherwise has a legitimate business need for the information in connection with a business transaction involving the consumer.

"Sec. 605. Obsolete information

"(a) Except as authorized under subsection (b), no consumer reporting agency may make any consumer report containing any of the following items of information:

"(1) Cases under title 11 of the United States Code or under the Bankruptcy Act that, from the date of entry of the order for relief or the date of adjudication, as the cause may be, antedate the report by more than 10 years.

"(2) Suits and judgments which, from date of entry, antedate the report by more than seven years or until the governing statute of limitations has expired, whichever is the longer period.

"(3) Paid tax liens which, from date of payment, antedate the report by more than seven years.

"(4) Accounts placed for collection or charged to profit and loss which antedate the report by more than seven years.

"(5) Records of arrest, indictment, or conviction of crime which, from date of disposition, release, or parole, antedate the report by more than seven years.

"(6) Any other adverse item of information which antedates the report by more than seven years.

"(b) The provisions of subsection (a) are not applicable in the case of any consumer credit report to be used in connection with--

"(1) a credit transaction involving, or which may reasonably be expected to involve, a principal amount of $50,000 or more;

"(2) the underwriting of life insurance involving, or which may reasonably be expected to involve, a face amount of $50,000 or more; or

"(3) the employment of any individual at an annual salary which equals, or which may reasonably be expected to equal $20,000, or more.

"Sec. 606. Disclosure of investigative consumer reports

"(a) A person may not procure or cause to be prepared an investigative consumer report on any consumer unless--

"(1) it is clearly and accurately disclosed to the consumer that an investigative consumer report including information as to his character, general reputation, personal characteristics, and mode of living, whichever are applicable, may be made, and such disclosure (A) is made in a writing mailed, or otherwise delivered, to the consumer, not later than three days after the date on which the report was first requested, and (B) includes a statement informing the consumer of his right to request the additional disclosures provided for under subsection (b) of this section; or

"(2) the report is to be used for employment purposes for which the consumer has not specifically applied.

"(b) Any person who procures or causes to be prepared an investigative consumer report on any consumer shall, upon written request made by the consumer within a reasonable period of time after the receipt by him of the disclosure required by subsection (a) (1), shall make a complete and accurate disclosure of the nature and scope of the investigation requested. This disclosure shall be made in a writing mailed, or otherwise delivered, to the consumer not later than five days after the date on which the request for such disclosure was received from the consumer or such report was first requested, whichever is the later.

"(c) No person may be held liable for any violation of subsection (a) or (b) of this section if he shows by a preponderance of the evidence that at the time of the violation he maintained reasonable procedures to assure compliance with subsection (a) or (b).

"Sec. 607. Compliance procedures

"(a) Every consumer reporting agency shall maintain reasonable procedures designed to avoid violations of section 605 and to limit the furnishing of consumer reports to the purposes listed under section 604. These procedures shall require that prospective users of the information identify themselves, certify the purposes for which the information is sought, and certify that the information will be used for no other purpose. Every consumer reporting agency shall make a reasonable effort to verify the identity of a new prospective user and the uses certified by such prospective user prior to furnishing such user a consumer report. No consumer reporting agency may furnish a consumer report to any person if it has reasonable grounds for believing that the consumer report will not be used for a purpose listed in section 604.

"(b) Whenever a consumer reporting agency prepares a consumer report it shall follow reasonable procedures to assure maximum possible accuracy of the information concerning the individual about whom the report relates.

"Sec. 608. Disclosures to governmental agencies

"Notwithstanding the provisions of section 604, a consumer reporting agency may furnish identifying information respecting any consumer, limited to his name, address, former addresses, places of employment, or former places of employment, to a governmental agency.

"Sec. 609. Disclosures to consumers

"(a) Every consumer reporting agency shall, upon request and proper identification of any consumer, clearly and accurately disclose to the consumer:

"(1) The nature and substance of all information (except medical information) in its files on the consumer at the time of the request.

"(2) The sources of the information; except that the sources of information acquired solely for use in preparing an investigative consumer report and actually used for no other purpose need not be disclosed. Provided, That in the event an action is brought under this title, such sources shall be available to the plaintiff under appropriate discovery procedures in the court in which the action is brought.

"(3) The recipients of any consumer report on the consumer which it has furnished--

"(A) for employment purposes within the two-year period preceding the request, and

"(B) for any other purpose within the six-month period preceding the request.

"(b" The requirements of subsection (a) respecting the disclosure of sources of information and the recipients of consumer reports do not apply to information received or consumer reports furnished prior to the effective date of this title except to the extent that the matter involved is contained in the files of the consumer reporting agency on that date.

"Sec. 610. Conditions of disclosure to consumers

"(a) A consumer reporting agency shall make the disclosures required under section 609 during normal business hours and on reasonable notice.

"(b) The disclosures required under section 609 shall be made to the consumer--

"(1) in person if he appears in person and furnishes proper identification; or

"(2) by telephone if he has made a written request, with proper identification, for telephone disclosure and the toll charge, if any, for the telephone call is prepaid by or charged directly to the consumer.

"(c) Any consumer reporting agency shall provide trained personnel to explain to the consumer any information furnished to him pursuant to section 609.

"(d) The consumer shall be permitted to be accompanied by one other person of his choosing, who shall furnish reasonable identification. A consumer reporting agency may require the consumer to furnish a written statement granting permission to the consumer reporting agency to discuss the consumer's file in such person's presence.

"(e) Except as provided in sections 616 and 617, no consumer may bring any action or proceeding in the nature of defamation, invasion of privacy, or negligence with respect to the reporting of information against any consumer reporting agency, any user of information, or any person who furnishes information to a consumer reporting agency, based on informa- tion disclosed pursuant to section 609, 610 or 615, except as to false information furnished with malice or willful intent to injure such consumer.

"Sec. 611. Procedure in case of disputed accuracy

"(a) If the completeness or accuracy of any item of information contained in his file is disputed by a consumer, and such dispute is directly conveyed to the consumer reporting agency by the consumer, the consumer reporting agency shall within a reasonable period of time reinvestigate and record the current status of that information unless it has reasonable grounds to believe that the dispute by the consumer is frivolous or irrelevant. If after such reinvestigation such information is found to be inaccu rate or can no longer be verified, the consumer reporting agency shall promptly delete such information. The presence of contradictory information in the consumer's file does not in and of itself constitute reasonable grounds for believing the dispute is frivolous or irrelevant.

"(b) If the reinvestigation does not resolve the dispute, the consumer may file a brief statement setting forth the nature of the dispute. The consumer reporting agency

220

may limit such statements to not more than one hundred words if it provides the consumer with assistance in writing a clear summary of the dispute.

"(c) Whenever a statement of a dispute is filed, unless there is reasonable grounds to believe that it is frivolous or irrelevant, the consumer reporting agency shall, in any subsequent consumer report containing the information in question, clearly note that it is disputed by the consumer and provide either the consumer's statement or a clear and accurate codification or summary thereof.

"(d) Following any deletion of information which is found to be inaccurate or whose accuracy can no longer be verified or any notation as to disputed information, the consumer reporting agency shall, at the request of the consumer, furnish notification that the item has been deleted or the statement, codification or summary pursuant to subsection (b) or (c) to any person specifically designated by the consumer who has within two years prior thereto received a consumer report for employment purposes, or within six months prior thereto received a consumer report for any other purpose, which contained the deleted or disputed information. The consumer reporting agency shall clearly and conspicuously disclose to the consumer his rights to make such a request. Such disclosure shall be made at or prior to the time the information is deleted or the consumer's statement regarding the disputed information is received.

"Sec. 612. Charges for certain disclosures

"A consumer reporting agency shall make all disclosures pursuant to section 609 and furnish all consumer reports pursuant to section 611 (d) without charge to the consumer if, within thirty days after receipt by such consumer of a notification pursuant to section 615 or notification from a debt collection agency affiliated with such consumer reporting agency stating that the consumer's credit rating may be or has been adversely affected, the consumer makes a request under section 609 or 611 (d). Otherwise, the consumer reporting agency may impose a reasonable charge on the consumer for making disclosure to such consumer pursuant to section 609, the charge for which shall be indicated to the consumer prior to making disclosure; and for furnishing notifications, statements, summaries, or codifications to person designated by the consumer pursuant to section 611 (d), the charge for which shall be indicated to the consumer prior to furnishing such information, and shall not exceed the charge that the consumer reporting agency would impose on each designated recipient for a consumer report except that no charge may be made for notifying such persons of the deletion of information which is found to be inaccurate or which can no longer be verified.

"Sec. 613. Public record information for employment purposes
"A consumer reporting agency which furnishes a consumer report for employment purposes and which for that purpose compiles and reports items of information on consumers which are matters of public record and are likely to have an adverse effect upon a consumer's ability to obtain employment shall--

"(1) at the time such public record information is reported to the user of such consumer report, notify the consumer of the fact that public record information is being reported by the consumer reporting agency, together with the name and address of the person to whom such information is being reported; or

"(2) maintain strict procedures designed to insure that whenever public record information which is likely to have an adverse effect on a consumer's ability to obtain employment is reported it is complete and up to date. For purposes of this paragraph, items of public record relating to arrest, indictments, convictions, suits, tax liens, and outstanding judgments shall be considered up to date if the current public record status of the item at the time of the report is reported.

"Sec. 614. Restrictions on investigative consumer reports

"Whenever a consumer reporting agency prepares an investigative consumer report, no adverse information in the consumer report (other than information which is a matter of public record) may be included in a subsequent consumer report unless such adverse information has been verified in the process of making such subsequent consumer report, or the adverse information was received within the three-month period preceding the date the subsequent report is furnished.

"Sec. 615. Requirements on users of consumer reports

"(a) Whenever credit or insurance for personal, family, or household purposes, or employment involving a consumer is denied or the charge for such credit or insurance is increased either wholly or partly because of information contained in a consumer report from a consumer reporting agency, the user of the consumer report shall so advise the consumer against whom such adverse action has been taken and supply the name and address of the consumer reporting agency making the report.

"(b) Whenever credit for personal, family, or household purposes involving a consumer is denied or the charge for such credit is increased either wholly or partly because of information obtained from a person other than a consumer reporting agency bearing upon the consumer's credit worthiness, credit standing, credit capacity, character, general reputation, personal characteristics, or mode of living, the user of such information shall, within a reasonable period of time, upon the consumer's written request for the reasons for such adverse action received within sixty days after learning of such adverse action, disclose the nature of the information to the consumer. The user of such information shall clearly and accurately disclose to the consumer his right to make such written requests at the time such adverse action is communicated to the consumer.

"(c) No person shall be held liable for any violation of this section if he shows by a preponderance of the evidence that at the time of the alleged violation he maintained reasonable procedures to assure compliance with the provisions of subsections (a) and (b).

"Sec. 616. Civil liability for willful noncompliance

"Any consumer reporting agency or user of information which willfully fails to comply with any requirement imposed under this title with respect to any consumer is liable to that consumer in an amount equal to the sum of--

"(1) any actual damages sustained by the consumer as a result of the failure;

"(2) such amount of punitive damages as the court may allow; and

"(3) in the case of any successful action to enforce any liability under this section, the costs of the action together with reasonable attorney's fees as determined by the court.

"Sec. 617. Civil liability for negligent noncompliance

"Any consumer reporting agency or user of information which is negligent in failing to comply with any requirement imposed under this title with respect to any consumer is liable to that consumer in an amount equal to the sum of--

"(1) any actual damages sustained by the consumer as a result of the failure;

"(2) in the case of any successful action to enforce any liability under this section, the costs of the action together with reasonable attorney's fees as determined by the court.

"Sec. 618. Jurisdiction of courts; limitation of actions

"An action to enforce any liability created under this title may be brought in any appropriate United States district court without regard to the amount in controversy, or in any other court of competent jurisdiction, within two years from the date on which the liability arises, except that where a defendant has materially and willfully misrepresented any information required under this title to be disclosed to an individual and the information so misrepresented is material to the establishment of the defendant's liability to that individual under this title, the action may be brought at any time within two years after discovery by the individual of the misrepresentation.

"Sec. 619. Obtaining information under false pretenses

"Any person who knowingly and willfully obtains information on a consumer from a consumer reporting agency under false pretense shall be fined not more than $5,000 or imprisoned not more than one year, or both.

"Sec. 620. Unauthorized disclosures by officers or employees

"Any officer or employee of a consumer reporting agency who knowingly and willfully provides information concerning an individual from the agency's files to a person not authorized to receive that information shall be fined not more than $5,000 or imprisoned not more than one year, or both.

"Sec. 621. Administrative enforcement

"(a) Compliance with the requirements imposed under this title shall be enforced under the Federal Trade Commission Act by the Federal Trade Commission with respect to consumer reporting agencies and all other persons subject thereto, except to the extent that enforcement of the requirements imposed under this title is specifically committed to some other government agency under subsection (b) hereof. For the purpose of the exercise by the Federal Trade Commission Act, a violation of any requirement or prohibition imposed under this title shall constitute an unfair or deceptive act or practice in commerce in violation of section 5 (a) of the Federal Trade Commission pursuant to this subsection, irrespective of whether that person is engaged in commerce or meets any other jurisdictional tests in the Federal Trade Commission Act. The Federal Trade Commission shall have such procedural, investigative, and enforcement powers, including the power to issue procedural rules in enforcing compliance with the requirements imposed under this title and to require the filing of reports, the production of documents, and the appearance of witnesses as though the applicable terms and conditions of the Federal Trade Commission Act were part of this title. Any person violating any of the provisions of this title shall be subject to the penalties and entitled to the privileges and immunities provided in the Federal Trade Commission Act as though the applicable terms and provisions thereof were part of this title.

"(b) Compliance with the requirements imposed under this title with respect to consumer reporting agencies and persons who use consumer reports from such agencies shall be enforced under--

"(1) section 8 of the Federal Deposit Insurance Act, in the case of:

"(A) national banks, by the Comptroller of the Currency;

"(B) member banks of the Federal Reserve Board; and

"(C) banks insured by the Federal Deposit Insurance Corporation (other than members of the Federal Reserve System), by the Board of Directors of the Federal Deposit Insurance Corporation.

"(2) section 5 (d) of the Home Owners Loan Act of 1933, section 407 of the National Housing Act, and sections 6 (i) and 17 of the Federal Home Loan Bank Act, by the Federal Home Loan Bank Board (acting directly or through the Federal Savings and Loan Insurance Corporation), in the case of any institution subject to any of those provisions;

"(3) the Federal Credit Union Act, by the Administrator of the National Credit Union Administration with respect to any Federal credit union;

"(4) the Acts to regulate commerce, by the Interstate Commerce Commission with respect to any common carrier subject to those Acts;

"(5) the Federal Aviation Act of 1958, by the Civil Aeronautics Board with respect to any air carrier or foreign air carrier subject to that Act; and

"(6) the Packers and Stockyards Act, 1921 (except as provided in section 406 of that Act), by the Secretary of Agriculture with respect to any activities subject to that Act.

"(c) For the purpose of the exercise by any agency referred to in subsection (b) of its powers under any Act referred to in that subsection, a violation of any requirement imposed under this title shall be deemed to be a violation of a requirement imposed under that Act. In addition to its powers under any provision of law specifically referred to in that subsection may exercise, for the purpose of enforcing compliance with any requirement imposed under this title any other authority conferred on it by law.

"Sec. 622.   Relation to State laws

"This title does not annul, alter, affect, or exempt any person subject to the provisions of this title from complying with the laws of any State with respect to the collection, distribution, or use of any information on consumers, except to the extent that those laws are inconsistent with any provision of this title, and then only to the extent of the inconsistency."

EFFECTIVE DATE

Sec. 602. Section 504 of the Consumer Credit Protection Act is amended by adding at the end thereof the following new subsection:

"(d) Title VI takes effect upon the expiration of one hundred and eighty days following the date of its enactment."

And the Senate agree to the same.

TITLE III--FAIR CREDIT BILLING

"Sec. 301. Short title
This title may be cited as the "Fair Credit Billing Act".

"Sec. 302. Declaration of purpose
The last sentence of section 102 of the Truth in Lending Act (15 U.S.C.1601) is amended by striking out the period and inserting in lieu thereof a comma and the following: "and to protect the consumer against inaccurate and unfair credit billing and credit card practices."

'Sec. 303. Definitions of creditor and open end credit plan
The first sentence of section 103 (f) of the Truth in Lending Act (15 U.S.C. 1602 (f)) is amended to read as follows: "The term 'creditor' refers only to creditors who regularly extend, or arrange for the extension of, credit which is payable by agreement in more than four installments or for which the payment of a finance charge is or may be required, whether in connection with loans, sales of property or services, or otherwise. For the purposes of the requirements imposed under Chapter 4 and sections 127 (a)(6), 127 (a)(7), 127 (a)(8), 127 (b)(1), 127 (b)(2), 127 (b)(3), 127 (b)(9), and 127 (b)(11) of Chapter 2 of this Title, the term 'creditor' shall also include card issuers whether or not the amount due is payable by agreement in more than four installments or the payment of a finance charge is or may be required, and the Board shall, by regulation, apply these requirements to such card issuers, to the extent appropriate, even though the requirements are by their terms applicable only to creditors offering open end credit plans.

"Sec. 304. Disclosure of fair credit billing rights
"(a) Section 127 (a) of the Truth in Lending Act (15 U.S.C. 1637 (a)) is amended by adding at the end thereof a new paragraph as follows:

"(8) A statement, in a form prescribed by regulations of the Board of the protection provided by sections 161 and 170 to an obligor and the creditor's responsibilities under sections 162 and 170. With respect to each of two billing cycles per year, at semiannual intervals, the creditor shall transmit such statement to each obligor to whom the creditor is required to transmit a statement pursuant to section 127 (b) for such billing cycle."

"(b) Section 127 (c) of such Act (15 U.S.C. 1637 (c)) is amended to read:

"(c) In the case of any existing account under an open end consumer credit plan having an outstanding balance of more than $1 at or after the close of the creditor's first full billing cycle under the plan after the effective date of subsection (a) or any amendments thereto, the items described in subsection (a), to the extent applicable and not previously disclosed, shall be disclosed in a notice mailed or delivered to the obligor not later than the time of mailing the next statement required by subsection (b)."

"Sec. 305. Disclosure of billing contact

Section 127 (b) of the Truth in Lending Act (15 U.S.C. 1637 (b)) is amended by adding at the end thereof a new paragraph as follows:

"(11) The address to be used by the creditor for the purpose of receiving billing inquiries from the obligor."

"Sec. 306. Billing practices

The Truth in Lending Act (15 U.S.C. 1601-1665) is amended by adding at the end thereof a new chapter as follows:

"Chapter 4--CREDIT BILLING'

"Sec. 161. Correction of billing errors:

"(a) If a creditor, within sixty days after having transmitted to an obligor a statement of the obligor's account in connection with an extension of consumer credit, receives at the address disclosed under section 127 (b)(11) a written notice (other than notice on a payment stub or other payment medium supplied by the creditor if the creditor so stipulates with the disclosure required under section 127 (a)(8)) from the obligor in which the obligor--

"(1) sets forth or otherwise enables the creditor to identify the name and account number (if any) of the obligor,

"(2) indicates the obligor's belief that the statement contains a billing error and the amount of such billing error, and

"(3) sets forth the reasons for the obligor's belief (to the extent applicable) that the statement contains a billing error, the creditor shall, unless the obligor has, after giving such written notice and before the expiration of the time limits herein specified, agreed that the statement was correct--

"(A) not later than thirty days after the receipt of the notice, send a written acknowledgement thereof to the obligor, unless the action required in sub-paragraph (B) is taken within such thirty-day period, and

"(B) not later than two complete billing cycles of the creditor (in no event later than ninety days) after the receipt of the notice and prior to taking any action to collect the amount, or any part thereof, indicated by the obligor under paragraph (2) either--

"(i) make appropriate corrections in the account of this obligor, including the crediting of any finance charges on amounts erroneously billed, and transmit to the obligor a notification of such corrections and the creditor's explanation of any change in the amount indicated by the obligor under paragraph (2) and, if any such change is made and the obligor so requests, copies of documentary evidence of the obligor's indebtedness; or "(ii) send a written explanation or clarification to the obligor, after having conducted an investigation, setting forth to the extent applicable the reasons why the creditor believes the account of the obligor was correctly shown in the statement and, upon request of the obligor, provide copies of documentary evidence of the obligor's indebtedness. In the case of a billing error where the obligor alleges that the creditor's billing statement reflects goods not delivered to the obligor or his designee in accordance with the agreement made at the time of the transaction, a creditor may not construe such amount to be correctly shown unless he determines that such goods were actually delivered, mailed, or otherwise sent to the obligor and provides the obligor with a statement of such determination.

After complying with the provisions of this subsection with respect to an alleged billing error, a creditor has no further responsibility under this section if the obligor continues to make substantially the same allegation with respect to such error.

"(b) For the purpose of this section, a 'billing error' consists of any of the following:

"(1) A reflection on a statement of an extension of credit which was not made to the obligor or, if made, was not in the amount reflected on such statement.

"(2) A reflection on a statement of an extension of credit for which the obligor requests additional clarification including documentary evidence thereof.

"(3) A reflection on a statement of goods or services not accepted by the obligor or his designee or not delivered to the obligor or his designee in accordance with the agreement made at the time of a transaction.

"(4) The creditor's failure to reflect properly on a statement a payment made by the obligor or a credit issued to the obligor.

"(5) A computation error or similar error of an accounting nature of the creditor on a statement.

"(6) Any other error described in regulations of the Board.

"(c) For the purposes of this section, 'action to collect the amount', or any part thereof, indicated by an obligor under paragraph (2) does not include the sending of statements of account to the obligor following written notice from the obligor as specified under subsection (a), if--

"(1) the obligor's account is not restricted or closed because of the failure of the obligor to pay the amount indicated under paragraph (2) of subsection (a), and

"(2) the creditor indicates the payment of such amount is not required pending the creditor's compliance with this section.

Nothing in this section shall be construed to prohibit any action by a creditor to collect any amount which has not been indicated by the obligor to contain a billing error.

"(d) Pursuant to regulations of the Board, a creditor operating an open end consumer credit plan may not, prior to the sending of the written explanation or clarification required under paragraph (B) (ii), restrict or close an account with respect to which the obligor has indicated pursuant to subsection (a) that he believes such account to contain a billing error solely because of the obligor's failure to pay the amount indicated to be in error. Nothing in this subsection shall be deemed to prohibit a creditor from applying against the credit limit on the obligor's account the amount indicated to be in error.

"(e) Any creditor who fails to comply with the requirements of this section or section 162 forfeits any right to collect from the obligor the amount indicated by the obligor under paragraph (2) of subsection (a) of this section, and any finance charges thereon, except that the amount required to be forfeited under this subsection may not exceed $50.

"Sec. 162. Regulation of credit reports

"(a) After receiving a notice from an obligor as provided in section 161 (a), a creditor or his agent may not directly or indirectly threaten to report to any person adversely on the obligor's credit rating or credit standing because of the obligor's failure to pay the amount indicated by the obligor under section 161 (a)(2), and such amount may not be reported as delinquent to any third party until the creditor has met the requirements of section 161 and has allowed the obligor the same number of days (not less than ten) thereafter to make payment as is provided under the credit agreement with the obligor for the payment of undisputed amounts.

"(b) If a creditor receives a further written notice from an obligor that an amount is still in dispute within the time allowed for payment under subsection (a) of this section, a creditor may not report to any third party that the amount of the obligor is delinquent because the obligor has failed to pay an amount which he has indicated under section 161 (a)(2), unless the creditor also reports that the amount is in dispute and, at the same time, notifies the obligor of the name and address of each party to whom the creditor is reporting information concerning the delinquency.

"(c) A creditor shall report any subsequent resolution of any delinquencies reported pursuant to subsection (b) to the parties to whom such delinquencies were initially reported.

"Sec. 163. Length of billing period

"(a) If an open end consumer credit plan provides a time period within which an obligor may repay any portion of the credit extended without incurring an additional finance charge, such additional finance charge may not be imposed with respect to such portion of the credit extended for the billing cycle of which such period is a part unless a statement which includes the amount upon which the finance charge for that period is based was mailed at least fourteen days prior to the date specified in the statement by which payment must be made in order to avoid imposition of that finance charge.

"(b) Subsection (a) does not apply in any case where a creditor has been prevented, delayed, or hindered in making timely mailing or delivery of such periodic statement within the time period specified in such subsection because of an act of God, war, natural disaster, strike, or other excusable or justifiable cause, as determined under regulations of the Board.

"Sec. 164. Prompt crediting of payments

"Payments received from an obligor under an open end consumer credit plan by the creditor shall be posted promptly to the obligor's account as specified in regulations of the Board. Such regulations shall prevent a finance charge from being imposed on any obligor if the creditor has received the obligor's payment in readily identifiable form in the amount, manner, location, and time indicated by the credit to avoid the imposition thereof.

"Sec. 165. Crediting excess payments

"Whenever an obligor transmits funds to a creditor in excess of the total balance due on an open end consumer credit account, the creditor shall promptly (1) upon request of the obligor refund the amount of the overpayment, or (2) credit such amount to the obligor's account.

"Sec. 166. Prompt notification of returns

"With respect to any sales transaction where a credit card has been used to obtain credit, where the seller is a person other than the card issuer, and where the seller accepts or allows a return of the goods or forgiveness of a debit for services which were the subject of such sale, the seller shall promptly transmit to the credit card issuer, a credit statement with respect thereto and the credit card issuer shall credit the account of the obligor for the amount of the transaction.

"Sec. 167. Use of cash discounts

"(a) With respect to credit card which may be used for extensions of credit in sales transactions in which the seller is a person other than the card issuer; the card issuer may not, by contract or otherwise, prohibit any such seller from offering a discount to a cardholder to induce the cardholder to pay by cash, check, or similar means rather than use a credit card.

"(b) With respect to any sales transaction, and discount not in excess of 5 per centum offered by the seller for the purpose of inducing payment by cash, check, or other means not involving the use of a credit card shall not constitute a finance charge as determined under section 106, if such discount is offered to all prospective buyers and its availability is disclosed to all prospective buyers clearly and conspicuously in accordance with regulations of the Board.

"Sec. 168. Prohibition of tie-in services

"Notwithstanding any agreement to the contrary, a card issuer may not require a seller, as a condition to participating in a credit card plan, to open an account with or procure any other service from the card issuer or its subsidiary or agent.

"Sec. 169. Prohibition of offsets

"(a) A card issuer may not take any action to offset a cardholder's indebtedness arising in connection with a consumer credit transaction under the relevant credit card plan against funds of the cardholder held on deposit with the card issuer unless--

"(1) such action was previously authorized in writing by the cardholder in accordance with a credit plan whereby the cardholder agrees periodically to pay debts incurred in his open end credit account by permitting the card issuer periodically to deduct all or a portion of such debt from the cardholder's deposit account, and

"(2) such action with respect to any outstanding disputed amount not be taken by the card issuer upon request of the cardholder.

In the case of any credit card account in existence on the effective date of this section, the previous written authorization referred to in clause (1) shall not be required until the date (after such effective date) when such account is renewed, but in no case later than one year after such effective date. Such written authorization shall be deemed to exist if the card issuer has previously notified the cardholder that the use of his credit card account will subject any funds which the card issuer holds in deposit accounts of such cardholder to offset against any amounts due and payable on his credit card account which have not been paid in accordance with the terms of the agreement between the card issuer and the cardholder.

"(b) This section does not alter or affect the right under State law of a card issuer to attach or otherwise levy upon funds of a cardholder held on deposit with the card issuer if that remedy is constitutionally available to creditors generally.

"Sec. 170. Rights of credit card customers

"(a) Subject to the limitation contained in subsection (b), a card issuer who has issued a credit card to a cardholder pursuant to an open end consumer credit plan shall be subject to all claims (other than tort claims) and defenses arising out of any transaction in which the credit card is used as a method of payment or extension of credit if (1) the obligor has made a good faith attempt to obtain satisfactory resolution of a disagreement or problem relative to the transaction from the person honoring the credit card; (2) the amount of the initial transaction exceeds $50; and (3) the place where the initial transaction occurred was in the same State as the mailing address previously provided by the cardholder or was within 100 miles from such address, except that the limitations set forth in clauses (2) and (3) with respect to an obligor's right to asset claims and defenses against a card issuer shall not be applicable to any transaction in which the person honoring the credit card (A) is the same person as the card issuer, (B) is controlled by the card issuer, (C) is under direct or indirect common control with the card issuer, (D) is a franchised dealer in the card issuer's products or services, or (E) has obtained the order for such transaction through a mail solicitation made by or participated in by the card issuer in which the cardholder is solicited to enter into such transaction by using the credit card issued by the card issuer.

"(b) The amount of claims or defenses asserted by the cardholder may not exceed the amount of credit outstanding with respect to such transaction at the time the cardholder first notifies the card issuer or the person honoring the credit card of such claim or defense. For the purpose of determining the amount of credit outstanding in the preceding sentence, payments and credits to the cardholder's account are deemed to have been applied, in the order indicated, to the payment of: (1) late charges in the order of their entry to the account; (2) finance charges in order of their entry to the account; and (3) debits to the account other than those set forth above, in the order in which each debit entry to the account was made.

"Sec. 171. Relation to State laws

"(a) This chapter does not annul, alter, or affect, or exempt any person subject to the provisions of this chapter from complying with, the laws of any State with respect to credit billing practices, except to the extent that those laws are inconsistent with any provision of this chapter, and then only to the extent of the inconsistency. The Board may not determine that any State law is inconsistent with any provision of this chapter if the Board determines that such law gives greater protection to the consumer.

"(b) The Board shall by regulation exempt from the requirements of this chapter any class of credit transactions within any State if it determines that under the law of that State that class of transactions is subject to requirements substantially similar to those imposed under this chapter or that such law gives greater protection to the consumer, and that there is adequate provision for enforcement."

CONSUMER CREDIT PROTECTION ACT

PUBLIC LAW 90-321; 82 STAT. 146

An Act to safeguard the consumer in connection with the utilization of credit by requiring full disclosure of the terms and conditions of finance charges in credit transactions or in offers to extend credit; by restricting the garnishment of wages; and by creating the National Commission on Consumer Finance to study and make recommendations on the need for further regulation of the consumer finance industry; and for other purposes.

Be it enacted by the Senate and House of Representatives of the United States of America in Congress assembled, That:

"Sec. 1. Short title of entire Act
This Act may be cited as the Consumer Credit Protection Act.

TITLE I--CONSUMER CREDIT COST DISCLOSURE

CHAPTER 1.--GENERAL PROVISIONS

"Sec. 101. Short title
This title may be cited as the Truth in Lending Act.

"Sec. 102. Findings and declaration of purpose
The Congress finds that economic stabilization would be enhanced and the competition among the various financial institutions and other firms engaged in the extension of consumer credit would be strengthened by the informed use of credit. The informed use of credit results from an awareness of the cost thereof by consumers. It is the purpose of this title to assure a meaningful disclosure of credit terms so that the consumer will be able to compare more readily the various credit terms available to him and avoid the uninformed use of credit.

"Sec. 103. Definitions and rules of construction

"(a) The definitions and rules of construction set forth in this section are applicable for the purposes of this title.

"(b) The term 'Board' refers to the Board of Governors of the Federal Reserve System.

"(c) The term 'organization' means a corporation, government or governmental subdivision or agency, trust, estate, partnership, cooperative, or association.

"(d) The term 'person' means a natural person or an organization.

"(e) The term 'credit' means the right granted by a creditor to a debtor to defer payment of debt or to incur debt and defer its payment.

"(f) The term 'creditor' refers only to creditors who regularly extend, or arrange for the extension of, credit for which the payment of a finance charge is required, whether in connection with loans, sales of property or services, or otherwise. The provisions of this title apply to any such creditor, irrespective of his or its status as a natural person or any type of organization.

"(g) The term 'credit sale' refers to any sale with respect to which credit is extended or arranged by the seller. The term includes any contract in the form of a bailment or lease if the bailee or lessee contracts to pay as compensation for use a sum substantially equivalent to or in excess of the aggregate value of the property and services involved and it is agreed that the bailee or lessee will become, or for no other or a nominal consideration has the option to become, the owner of the property upon full compliance with his obligations under the contract.

"(h) The adjective 'consumer', used with reference to a credit transaction, characterizes the transaction as one in which the party to whom credit is offered or extended is a natural person, and the money, property, or services which are the subject of the transaction are primarily for personal, family, household, or agricultural purposes.

"(i) The term 'open end credit plan' refers to a plan prescribing the terms of credit transactions which may be made thereunder from time to time and under the terms of which a finance charge may be computed on the outstanding unpaid balance from time to time thereunder.

"(j) The term 'State' refers to any State, the Commonwealth of Puerto Rico, the District of Columbia, and any territory or possession of the United States.

"(k) Any reference to any requirement imposed under this title or any provision thereof includes reference to the regulations of the Board under this title or the provision thereof in question.

"(l) The disclosure of an amount or percentage which is greater than the amount or percentage required to be disclosed under this title does not in itself constitute a violation of this title.

"Sec. 104. Exempted transactions

This title does not apply to the following:

"(1) Credit transactions involving extensions of credit for business or commercial purposes, or to government or governmental agencies or instrumentalities, or to organizations.

"(2) Transactions in securities or commodities accounts by a broker-dealer registered with the Securities and Exchange Commission.

"(3) Credit transactions, other than real property transactions, in which the total amount to be financed exceeds $25,000.

"(4) Transactions under public utility tariffs, if the Board determines that a State regulatory body regulates the charges for the public utility services involved, the charges for delayed payment, and any discount allowed for early payment.

"Sec. 105. Regulations

The Board shall prescribe regulations to carry out the purposes of this title. These regulations may contain such classifications, differentiations, or other provisions, and may provide for such adjustments and exceptions for any class of transactions, as in the judgment of the Board are necessary or proper to effectuate the purposes of this title, to prevent circumvention or evasion thereof, or to facilitate compliance therewith.

"Sec. 106. Determination of finance charge

"(a) Except as otherwise provided in this section, the amount of the finance charge in connection with any consumer credit transaction shall be determined as the sum of all charges, payable directly or indirectly by the person to whom the credit is extended, and imposed directly or indirectly by the creditor as an incident to the extension of credit, including any of the following types of charges which are applicable:

"(1) Interest, time price differential, and any amount payable under a point, discount, or other system of additional charges.

"(2) Service or carrying charge.

"(3) Loan fee, finder's fee, or similar charge.

"(4) Fee for an investigation or credit report.

"(5) Premium or other charge for any guarantee or insurance protecting the creditor against the obligor's default or other credit loss.

"(b) Charges or premiums for credit life, accident, or health insurance written in connection with any consumer credit transaction shall be included in the finance charge unless

"(1) the coverage of the debtor by the insurance is not a factor in the approval by the creditor of the extension of credit, and this fact is clearly disclosed in writing to the person applying for or obtaining the extension of credit; and

"(2) in order to obtain the insurance in connection with the extension of credit, the person to whom the credit is extended must give specific affirmative written indication of his desire to do so after written disclosure to him of the cost thereof.

"(c) Charges or premiums for insurance, written in connection with any consumer credit transaction, against loss of or damage to property or against liability arising out of the ownership or use of property, shall be included in the finance charge unless a clear and specific statement in writing is furnished by the creditor to the person to whom the credit is extended, setting forth the cost of the insurance if obtained from or through the creditor, and stating that the person to whom the credit is extended may choose the person through which the insurance is to be obtained.

"(d) If any of the following items is itemized and disclosed in accordance with the regulations of the Board in connection with any transaction, then the creditor need not include that item in the computation of the finance charge with respect to that transaction:

"(1) Fees and charges prescribed by law which actually are or will be paid to public officials for determining the existence of or for perfecting or releasing or satisfying any security related to the credit transaction.

"(2) The premium payable for an insurance in lieu of perfecting any security interest otherwise required by the creditor in connection with the transaction, if the premium does not exceed the fees and charges described in paragraph (1) which would otherwise be payable.

"(3) Taxes.

"(4) Any other type of charge which is not for credit and the exclusion of which from the finance charge is approved by the Board by regulation.

"(e) The following items, when charged in connection with any extension of credit secured by an interest in real property, shall not be included in the computation of the finance charge with respect to that transaction:

"(1) Fees or premiums for title examination, title insurance, or similar purposes.

"(2) Fees for preparation of a deed, settlement statement, or other documents.

"(3) Escrows for future payments of taxes and insurance.

"(4) Fees for notarizing deeds and other documents.

"(5) Appraisal fees.

"(6) Credit reports.

"Sec. 107. Determination of annual percentage rate

"(a) The annual percentage rate applicable to any extension of consumer credit shall be determined, in accordance with the regulations of the Board,

"(1) in the case of any extension of credit other than under an open end credit plan, as

"(A) that nominal annual percentage rate which will yield a sum equal to the amount of the finance charge when it is applied to the unpaid balances of the amount financed, calculated according to the actuarial method of allocating payments made on a debt between the amount financed and the amount of the finance charge, pursuant to which a payment is applied first to the accumulated finance charge and the balance is applied to the unpaid amount financed; or

"(B) the rate determined by any method prescribed by the Board as a method which materially simplifies computation while retaining reasonable accuracy as compared with the rate determined under subparagraph (A).

"(2) in the case of any extension of credit under an open end credit plan, as the quotient (expressed as a percentage) of the total finance charge for the period to which it relates divided by the amount upon which the finance charge for that period is based, multiplied by the number of such periods in a year.

"(b) Where a creditor imposes the same finance charge for balances within a specified range, the annual percentage rate shall be computed on the median balance within the range, except that if the Board determines that a rate so computed would not be meaningful, or would be materially misleading, the annual percentage rate shall be computed on such other basis as the Board may by regulation required.

"(c) The annual percentage rate may be rounded to the nearest quarter of 1 per centum for credit transactions payable in substantially equal installments when a creditor determines the total finance charge on the basis of a single add-on, discount, periodic, or other rate, and the rate is converted into an annual percentage rate under procedures prescribed by the Board.

"(d) The Board may authorize the use of rate tables or charts which may provide for the disclosure of annual percentage rates which vary from the rate determined in accordance with subsection (a) (1) (A) by not more than such tolerances as the Board may allow. The Board may not allow a tolerance greater than 8 per centum of that rate except to simplify compliance where irregular payments are involved.

"(e) In the case of creditors determining the annual percentage rate in a manner other than as described in subsection (c) or (d), the Board may authorize other reasonable tolerances.

"(f) Prior to January 1, 1971, any rate required under this title to be disclosed as a percentage rate may, at the option of the creditor, be expressed in the form of the corresponding ratio of dollars per hundred dollars.

"Sec. 108.   Administrative enforcement

"(a) Compliance with the requirements imposed under this title shall be enforced under

"(1) section 8 of the Federal Deposit Insurance Act, in the case of

"(A) national banks, by the Comptroller of the Currency.

"(B) member banks of the Federal Reserve System (other than national banks), by the Board.

"(C) banks insured by the Federal Deposit Insurance Corporation (other (other than members of the Federal Reserve System), by the Board of Directors of the Federal Deposit Insurance Corporation.

"(2) section 5 (d) of the Home Owners' Loan Act of 1933, section 407 of the National Housing Act, and sections 6 (f) and 17 of the Federal Home Loan Bank Act, by the Federal Home Loan Bank Board (acting directly or through the Federal Savings and Loan Insurance Corporation), in the case of any institution subject to any of those provisions.

"(3) the Federal Credit Union Act, by the Director of the Bureau of Federal Credit Unions with respect to any Federal credit union.

"(4) the Acts to regulate commerce, by the Interstate Commerce Commission with respect to any common carrier subject to those Acts.

"(5) the Federal Aviation Act of 1958, by the Civil Aeronautics Board with respect to any air carrier or foreign air carrier subject to that Act.

"(6) the Packers and Stockyards Act, 1921 (except as provided in section 406 of that Act), by the Secretary of Agriculture with respect to any activities subject to that Act.

"(b) For the Purpose of the Exercise by any agency referred to in subsection (a) of its powers under any Act referred to in that subsection, a violation of any requirement imposed under this title shall be deemed to be a violation of any requirement imposed under this title shall be deemed to be a violation of a requirement imposed under that Act. In addition to its powers under any provision of law specifically referred to in subsection (a), each of the agencies referred to in that subsection may exercise, for the purpose of enforcing compliance with any requirement imposed under this title, any other authority conferred on it by law.

"(c) Except to the extent that enforcement of the requirements imposed under this title is specifically committed to some other Government agency under subsection (a), the Federal Trade Commission shall enforce such requirements. For the purpose of the exercise by the Federal Trade Commission of its functions and powers under the Federal Trade Commission Act, a violation of any requirement imposed under that Act. All of the functions and powers of the Federal Trade Commission under the Federal Trade Commission Act are available to the Commission to enforce complaince by any person with the requirements imposed under this title, irrespective of whether that person is engaged in commerce or meets any other jurisdictional tests in the Federal Trade Commission Act.

"(d) The authority of the Board to issue regulations under this title does not impair the authority of any other agency designated in this section to make rules respecting its own procedures in enforcing com- pliance with requirements imposed under this title.

"Sec. 109. Views of other agencies

In the exercise of its functions under this title, the Board may obtain upon request the views of any other Federal agency which, in the judgment of the Board, exercises regulatory or supervisory functions with respect to any class of creditors subject to this title.

"Sec. 110. Advisory committee

The Board shall establish an advisory committee to advise and consult with it in the exercise of its functions under this title. In appointing the members of the committee, the Board shall seek to achieve a fair representation of the interests of sellers of merchandise on credit, lenders, and the public. The committee shall meet from time to time at the call of the Board, and members thereof shall be paid transportation expenses and not to exceed $100 per diem.

"Sec. 111. Effect on other laws

"(a) This title does not annul, alter, or affect, or exempt any creditor from complying with, the laws of any State relating to the disclosure of information in connection with credit transactions, except to the extent that those laws are inconsistent with the provisions of this title or regulations thereunder, and then only to the extent of the inconsistency.

"(b) This title does not otherwise annul, alter or affect in any manner the meaning, scope or applicability of the laws of any State, including, but not limited to, laws relating to the types, amounts or rates of charges, or any element or elements of charges, permissible under such laws in connection with the extension or use of credit, nor does this title extend the applicability of those laws to any class of persons or transactions to which they would not otherwise apply.

"(c) In any action or proceeding in any court involving a consumer credit sale, the disclosure of the annual percentage rate as required under this title in connection with that sale may not be received as evidence that the sale was a loan or any type of transaction other than a credit sale.

"(d) Except as specified in sections 125 and 130, this title and the regulations issued thereunder do not affect the validity or enforceability of any contract or obligation under State or Federal law.

"Sec. 112. Criminal liability for willful and knowing violation

Whoever willfully and knowingly

"(1) gives false or inaccurate information or fails to provide information which he is required to disclose under the provisions of this title or any regulation issued thereunder,

"(2) uses any chart or table authorized by the Board under section 107 in such a manner as to consistently understate the annual percentage rate deterrmined under section 107 (a) (1) (A), or

"(3) otherwise fails to comply with any requirement imposed under this title, shall be fined not more than $5,000 or imprisoned not more than one year, or both.

"Sec. 113. Penalties inapplicable to governmental agencies

No civil or criminal penalty provided under this title for any violation thereof may be imposed upon the United States or any agency thereof, or upon any State or political subdivision thereof, or any agency of any State or political subdivision.

"Sec. 114. Reports by Board and Attorney General

Not later than January 3 of each year after 1969, the Board and the Attorney General shall, respectively, make reports to the Congress concerning the administration of their functions under this title, including such recommendations as the Board and the Attorney General, respectively, deem necessary or appropriate. In addition, each report of the Board shall include its assessment of the extent to which compliance with the requirements imposed under this title is being achieved.

CHAPTER 2--CREDIT TRANSACTIONS

"Sec. 121. General requirement of disclosure

"(a) Each creditor shall disclose clearly and conspicuously, in accordance with the regulations of the Board, to each person to whom con- sumer credit is extended and upon whom a finance charge is or may be imposed, the information required under this chapter.

"(b) If there is more than one obligor, a creditor need not furnish a statement of information required under this chapter to more than one of them.

"Sec. 122. Form of disclosure; additional information

"(a) Regulations of the Board need not require that disclosures pursuant to this chapter be made in the order set forth in this chapter, and may permit the use of terminology different from that employed in this chapter if it conveys substantially the same meaning.

"(b) Any creditor may supply additional information or explanations with any disclosures required under this chapter.

"Sec. 123. Exemption for State-regulated transactions

The Board shall by regulation exempt from the requirements of this chapter any class of credit transactions within any State if it determines that under the law of that State that class of transactions is subject to requirements substantially similar to those imposed under this chapter, and that there is adequate provision for enforcement.

"Sec. 124. Effect of subsequent occurrence

If information disclosed in accordance with this chapter is subsequently rendered inaccurate as the result of any act, occurrence, or agreement subsequent to the delivery of the required disclosures, the inaccuracy resulting therefrom does not constitute a violation of this chapter.

"Sec. 125. Right of rescission as to certain transactions

"(a) Except as otherwise provided in this section, in the case of any consumer credit transaction in which a security interest is retained or acquired in any real property which is used or is expected to be used as the residence of the person to whom credit is extended, the obligor shall have the right to rescind the transaction until midnight of the third business day following the consummation of the transaction or the delivery of the disclosures required under this section and all other material disclosures required under this chapter, whichever is later, by notifying the creditor, in accordance with regulations of the Board, of his intention to do so. The creditor shall clearly and conspicuously disclose, in accordance with regulations of the Board, to any obligor in a transaction subject to this section the rights of the obligor under this section. The creditor shall also provide, in accordance with regulations of the Board, an adequate opportunity to the obligor to exercise his right to rescind any transaction subject to this section.

"(b) When an obligor exercises his right to rescind under subsection (a), he is not liable for any finance or other charge, and any security interest given by the obligor becomes void upon such a rescission. Within ten days after receipt of a notice of rescission, the creditor shall return to the obligor any money or property given as earnest money, down-payment, or otherwise, and shall take any action necessary or appropriate to reflect the termination of any security interest created under the transaction. If the creditor has delivered any property to the obligor, the obligor may retain possession of it. Upon the performance of the creditor's obligations under this section, the obligor shall tender the property to the creditor, except that if return of the property in kind would be impracticable or inequitable, the obligor shall tender its reason- able value. Tender shall be made at the location of the property or at the residence of the obligor, at the option of the obligor. If the creditor does not take possession of the property within ten days after tender by the obligor, ownership of the property vests in the obligor without obligation on his part to pay for it.

"(c) Notwithstanding any rule of evidence, written acknowledgment of receipt of any disclosures required under this title by a person to whom a statement is required to be given pursuant to this section does no more than create a rebuttable presumption of delivery thereof.

"(d) The Board may, if it finds that such action is necessary in order to permit homeowners to meet bona fide personal financial emergencies, prescribe regulations authorizing the modification or waiver of any rights created under this section to the extent and under the circumstances set forth in those regulations.

(e) This section does not apply to the creation or retention of a first lien against a dwelling to finance the acquisition of that dwelling.

"Sec. 126. Content of periodic statements

If a creditor transmits periodic statements in connection with any extension of consumer credit other than under an open end consumer credit plan, then each of those statements shall set forth each of the following items:

"(1) The annual percentage rate of the total finance charge.

"(2) The date by which, or the period (if any) within which, payment must be made in order to avoid additional finance charges or other charges.

"(3) Such of the items set forth in section 127 (b) as the Board may be regulation require as appropriate to the terms and conditions under which the extension of credit in question is made.

"Sec. 127. Open end consumer credit plans

"(a) Before opening any account under an open end consumer credit plan, the creditor shall disclose to the person to whom credit is to be extended each of the following items, to the extent applicable:

"(1) The conditions under which a finance charge may be imposed, including the time period, if any, within which any credit extended may be repaid without incurring a finance charge.

"(2) The method of determining the balance upon which a finance charge will be imposed.

"(3) The method of determining the amount of the finance charge, including any minimum or fixed amount imposed as a finance charge.

"(4) Where one or more periodic rates may be used to compute the finance charge, each such rate, the range of balances to which it is applicable, and the corresponding nominal annual percentage rate determined by multiplying the periodic rate by the number of periods in a year.

"(5) If the creditor so elects,

"(A) the average effective annual percentage rate of return received from accounts under the plan for a representative period of time; or

"(B) whenever circumstances are such that the computation of a rate under subparagraph (A) would not be feasible or practical, or would be misleading or meaningless, a projected rate of return to be received from accounts under the plan.

The Board shall prescribe regulations, consistent with commonly accepted standards for accounting or statistical procedures, to carry out the purposes of this paragraph.

"(6) The conditions under which any other charges may be imposed, and the method by which they will be determined.

"(7) The conditions under which the creditor may retain or acquire any security interest in any property to secure the payment of any credit extended under the plan, and a description of the interest or interest which may be so retained or acquired.

"(b) The creditor of any account under an open end consumer credit plan shall transmit to the obligor, for each billing cycle at the end of which there is an outstanding balance in that account or with respect to which a finance charge is imposed, a statement setting forth each of the following items to the extent applicable:

"(1) The outstanding balance in the account at the beginning of the statement period.

"(2) The amount and date of each extension of credit during the period, and, if a purchase was involved, a brief identification (unless previously furnished) of the goods or services purchased.

"(3) The total amount credited to the account during the period.

"(4) The amount of any finance charge added to the account during the period, itemized to show the amounts, if any, due to the application of percentage rates and the amount, if any, imposed as a minimum or fixed charge.

"(5) Where one or more periodic rates may be used to compute the finance charge, each such rate, the range of balances to which it is applicable, and, unless the annual percentage rate (determined under section 107 (a) (2) is required to be disclosed pursuant to paragraph (6), the corresponding nominal annual percentage rate determined by multiplying the periodic rate by the number of periods in a year.

"(6) Where the total finance charge exceeds 50 cents for a monthly or longer billing cycle, or the pro rata part of 50 cents for a billing cycle shorter than monthly, the total finance charge expressed as an annual percentage rate (determined under section 107 (a) (2)), except that if the finance charge is the sum of two or more products of a rate times a portion of the balance, the creditor may, in lieu of disclosing a single rate for the total charge, disclose each such rate expressed as an annual percentage rate, and the part of the balance to which it is applicable.

"(7) At the election of the creditor, the average effective annual percentage rate of return (or the projected rate) under the plan as prescribed in subsection (a) (5).

"(8) The balance on which the finance charge was computed and a statement of how the balance was determined. If the balance is determined without first deducting all credits during the period, that fact and the amount of such payments shall also be disclosed.

"(9) The outstanding balance in the account at the end of the period.

"(10) The date by which, or the period (if any) within which, payment must be made to avoid additional finance charges.

"(c) In the case of any open end consumer credit plan in existence on the effective date of this subsection, the items described in subsection (a), to the extent applicable, shall be disclosed in a notice mailed or delivered to the obligor not later than thirty days after that date.

"Sec.   128.   Sales not under open end credit plans

"(a) In connection with each consumer credit sale not under an open end credit plan, the creditor shall disclose each of the following items which is applicable:

"(1) The cash price of the property or service purchased.

"(2) The sum of any amounts credited as downpayment (including any trade-in).

"(3) The difference between the amount referred to in paragraph (1) and the amount referred to in paragraph (2).

"(4) All other charges, individually itemized, which are included in the amount of the credit extended but which are not part of the finance charge.

"(5) The total amount to be financed (the sum of the amount described in paragraph (3) plus the amount described in paragraph (4).

"(6) Except in the case of a sale of a dwelling, the amount of the finance charge, which may in whole or in part be designated as a time-price differential or any similar term to the extent applicable.

"(7) The finance charge expressed as an annual percentage rate except in the case of a finance charge.

"(A) which does not exceed $5 and is applicable to an amount financed not exceeding $75, or

"(B) which does not exceed $7.50 and is applicable to an amount financed exceeding $75.

A creditor may not divide a consumer credit sale into two or more sales to avoid the disclosure of an annual percentage rate pursuant to this paragraph.

"(8) The number, amount, and due dates or periods of payments scheduled to repay the indebtedness.

"(9) The default, delinquency, or similar charges payable in the event of late payments.

"(10) A description of any security interest held or to be retained or identification of the property to which the security interest relates.

"(b) Except as otherwise provided in this chapter, the disclosures required under subsection (a) shall be made before the credit is extended, and may be made by disclosing the information in the contract or other evidence of indebtedness to be signed by the purchaser.

"(c) If a creditor receives a purchase order by mail or telephone without personal solicitation, and the cash price and the deferred payment price and the terms of financing, including the annual percentage rate, are set forth in the creditor's catalog or other printed material distributed to the public, then the disclosures required under subsection (a) may be made at any time not later than the date the first payment is due.

"(d) If a consumer credit sale is one of a series of consumer credit sales transactions made pursuant to an agreement providing for the addition of the deferred payment price of that sale to an existing outstanding balance, and the person to whom the credit is extended has approved in writing both the annual percentage rate or rates and the method of computing the finance charge or charges, and the creditor retains no security interest in any property as to which he has received payments aggregating the amount of the sales price including any finance charges attributable thereto, then the disclosure required under subsection (a) for the particular sale may be made at any time not later than the date the first payment for that sale is due. For the purposes of this subsection, in the case of items purchased on different dates, the first purchased shall be deemed first paid for, and in the case of items purchased on the same date, the lowest priced shall be deemed first paid for.

"Sec. 129.   Consumer loans not under open end credit plans

"(a)   Any creditor making a consumer loan or otherwise extending consumer credit in a transaction which is neither a consumer credit sale nor under an open end consumer credit plan shall disclose each of the following items, to the extent applicable:

"(1)   The amount of credit of which the obligor will have the actual use, or which is or will be paid to him or for his account or to another person on his behalf.

"(2)   All charges, individually itemized, which are included in the amount of credit extended but which are not part of the finance charge.

"(3)   The total amount to be financed (the sum of the amounts referred to in paragraph (1) plus the amounts referred to in paragraph (2)).

"(4)   Except in the case of a loan secured by a first lien on a dwelling and made to finance the purchase of that dwelling, the amount of the finance charge.

"(5)   The finance charge expressed as an annual percentage rate except in the case of a finance charge.

"(A)   which does not exceed $5 and is applicable to an extension of consumer credit not exceeding $75, or

"(B)   which does not exceed $7.50 and is applicable to an extension of consumer credit exceeding $75.

A creditor may not divide an extension of credit into two or more transactions to avoid the disclosure of an annual percentage rate pursuant to this paragraph.

"(6)   The number, amount, and the due dates or periods of payments scheduled to repay the indebtedness.

"(7)   The default, delinquency, or similar charges payable in the event of late payments.

"(8)   A description of any security interest held or to be retained or acquired by the creditor in connection with the extension of credit, and a clear identification of the property to which the security interest relates.

"(b)   Except as otherwise provided in this chapter, the disclosures required by subsection (a) shall be made before the credit is extended, and may be made by disclosing the information in the note or other evidence of indebtedness to be signed by the obligor.

"(c)   If a creditor receives a request for an extension of credit by mail or telephone without personal solicitation and the terms of financing, including the annual percentage rate for representative amounts of credit, are set forth in the creditor's printed material distributed to the public, or in the contract of loan or other printed material delivered to the obligor, then the disclosures required under subsection (a) may be made at any time not later than the date the first payment is due.

"Sec.   130.   Civil liability

'(a) Except as otherwise provided in this section, any creditor who fails in connection with any consumer credit transaction to disclose to any person any information required under this chapter to be disclosed to that person is liable to that person in an amount equal to the sum of

"(1) twice the amount of the finance charge in connection with the transaction, except that the liability under this paragraph shall not be less than $100 nor greater than $1,000; and

"(2) in the case of any successful action to enforce the foregoing liability, the costs of the action together with a reasonable attorney's fee as determined by the court.

"(b) A creditor has no liability under this section if within fifteen days after discovering an error, and prior to the institution of an action under this section or the receipt of written notice of the error, the creditor notifies the person concerned of the error and makes whatever adjustments in the appropriate account are necessary to insure that the person will not be required to pay a finance charge in excess of the amount or percentage rate actually disclosed.

"(c) A creditor may not be held liable in any action brought under this section for a violation of this chapter if the creditor shows by a preponderance of evidence that the violation was not intentional and resulted from a bona fide error notwithstanding the maintenance of procedures reasonably adapted to avoid any such error.

"(d) Any action which may be brought under this section against the original creditor in any credit transaction involving a security interest in real property may be maintained against any subsequent assignee of the original creditor where the assignee, its subsidiaries, or affiliates were in a continuing business relationship with the original creditor either at the time the credit was extended or at the time of the assignment, unless the assignment was involuntary, or the assignee shows by a preponderance of evidence that it did not have reasonable grounds to believe that the original creditor was engaged in violations of this chapter, and that it maintained procedures reasonably adapted to apprise it of the existence of any such violations.

"(e) Any action under this section may be brought in any United States district court, or in any other court of competent jurisdiction, within one year from the date of the occurrence of the violation.

"Sec. 131. Written acknowledgment as proof of receipt

Except as provided in section 125 (c) and except in the case of actions brought under section 130 (d), in any action or proceeding by or against any subsequent assignee of the original creditor without knowledge to the contrary by the assignee when he acquires the obligation, written acknowledgment of receipt by a person to whom a statement is required to be given pursuant to this title shall be conclusive proof of the delivery thereof and, unless the violation is apparent on the face of the delivery thereof and, unless the violation is apparent on the face of the statement, of compliance with this chapter. This section does not affect the rights of the obligor in any action against the original creditor.

CHAPTER 3--CREDIT ADVERTISING

"Sec. 141. Catalogs and multiple-page advertisements

For the purposes of this chapter, a catalog or other multiple-page advertisement shall be considered a single advertisement if it clearly and conspicuously displays a credit terms table on which the information required to be stated under this chapter is clearly set forth.

"Sec. 142. Advertising of downpayments and installments

No advertisement to aid, promote, or assist directly or indirectly any extension of consumer credit may state

"(1) that a specific periodic consumer credit amount or installment amount can be arranged, unless the creditor usually and customarily arranges credit payments or installments for that period and in that amount.

"(2) that a specified downpayment is required in connection with any extension of consumer credit, unless the creditor usually and customarily arranges downpayments in that amount.

"Sec. 143. Advertising of open end credit plans

No advertisement to aid, promote, or assist directly or indirectly the extension of consumer credit under an open end credit plan may set forth any of the specific terms of that plan or the appropriate rate determined under section 127 (a) (5) unless it also clearly and conspicuously sets forth all of the following items:

"(1) The time period, if any, within which any credit extended may be repaid without incurring a finance charge.

"(2) The method of determining the balance upon which a finance charge will be imposed.

"(3) The method of determining the amount of the finance charge, including any minimum or fixed amount imposed as a finance charge.

"(4) Where periodic rates may be used to compute the finance charge, the periodic rates expressed as annual percentage rates.

"(5) Such other or additional information for the advertising of open end credit plans as the Board may by regulation require to provide for adequate comparison of credit costs as between different types of open end credit plans.

"Sec. 144. Advertising of credit other than open end plans

"(a) Except as provided in subsection (b), this section applies to any advertisement to aid, promote, or assist directly or indirectly any consumer credit sale, loan, or other extension of credit subject to the provisoes of this title, other than open end credit plan.

"(b) The provisions of this section do not apply to advertisements of residential real estate except to the extent that the Board may be regulation require.

"(c) If any advertisement to which this section applies states the rate of a finance charge, the advertisement shall state the rate of that charge expressed as an annual percentage rate.

"(d) If any advertisement to which this section applies states the amount of the downpayment, if any, the amount of any installment payment, the dollar amount of any finance charge, or the number of installments or the period of repayment, then the advertisement shall state all of the following items:

      "(1) The cash price or the amount of the loan as applicable.

      "(2) The downpayment, if any.

      "(3) The number, amount, and due dates or period of payments scheduled to repay the indebtedness if the credit is extended.

      "(4) The rate of the finance charge expressed as an annual percentage rate.

"Sec. 145. Nonliability of media

There is no liability under this chapter on the part of any owner or personnel, as such, of any medium in which an advertisement appears or through which it is disseminated.

TITLE V - EQUAL CREDIT OPPORTUNITY

"Sec. 501. Short title
This title may be cited as the "Equal Credit Opportunity Act".

"Sec. 502. Findings and purpose
The Congress finds that there is a need to insure that the various financial institutions and other firms engaged in the extensions of credit exercise their responsibility to make credit available with fairness, impartiality, and without discrimination on the basis of sex or marital status. Economic stablization would be enhanced and competition among the various financial institutions and other firms engaged in the extension of credit would be strengthened by an absence of discrimination on the basis of sex and marital status, as well as by the informed use of credit which Congress has heretofore sought to promote. It is the purpose of this Act to require that financial institutions and other firms engaged in the extension of credit make the credit equally available to all creditworthy customers without regard to sex or marital status.

"Sec. 503.   Amendment to the Consumer Credit Protection Act
The Consumer Credit Protection Act (Public Law 90-321), is amended by adding at the end thereof a new title VII:

"TITLE VII - EQUAL CREDIT OPPORTUNITY

"Sec. 701.   Prohibited discrimination
"(a) It shall be unlawful for any creditor to discriminate against any applicant on the basis of sex or marital status with respect to any aspect of a credit transaction.

"(b) An inquiry of marital status shall not constitute discrimination for purposes of this title if such inquiry is for the purpose of ascertaining the creditor's rights and remedies applicable to the particular extension of credit, and not to discriminate in a determination of creditworthiness.

"Sec. 702. Definitions
"(a)   The definitions and rules of construction set forth in this section are applicable for the purposes of this title.

"(b) The term 'applicant' means any person who applies to a creditor directly for "(b) The term 'applicant' means any person who applies to a creditor directly for an extension, renewal, or continuation of credit, or applies to a creditor indirectly by use of an existing credit plan for an amount exceeding a previously established credit limit.

"(c) The term 'Board' refers to the Board of Governors of the Federal Reserve System.

"(d) The term 'credit' means the right granted by a creditor to a debtor to defer payment of debt or to incur debts and defer its payment or to purchase property or services and defer payment therefor.

"(e) The term 'creditor' means any person who regularly extends, renews, or continues credit; any person who regularly arranges for the extension, renewal, or continuation of credit; or any assignee of an original creditor who participates in the decision to extend, renew, or continue credit.

"(f) The term 'person' means a natural person, a corporation, government or governmental subdivision or agency, trust, estate, partnership, cooperative, or association.

"(g) Any reference to any requirement imposed under this title or any provision thereof includes reference to the regulations of the Board under this title or the provision thereof in question.

"Sec. 703. Regulations

"The Board shall also prescribe regulations to carry out the purposes of this title. These regulations may contain but are not limited to such classifications, differentiation, or other provision, and may provide for such adjustments and exceptions for any class of transactions, as in the judgment of the Board are necessary or proper to effectuate the purposes of this title, to prevent circumvention or evasion thereof, or to facilitate or substantiate compliance therewith. Such regulations shall be prescribed as soon as possible after the date of enactment of this Act, but in no event later than the effective date of this Act.

"Sec. 704. Administrative enforcement

"(a) Compliance with the requirements imposed under this title shall be enforced under:

"(A) national banks, by the Comptroller of the Currency,

"(B) member banks of the Federal Reserve System (other than national banks), by the Board,

"(C) banks insured by the Federal Deposit Insurance Corporation (other than members of the Federal Reserve System), by the Board of Directors of of Directors of the Federal Deposit Insurance Corporation.

"(2) Section 5 (d) of the Home Owners' Loan Act of 1933, section 407 of the National Housing Act, and sections 6 (i) and 17 of the Federal Home Loan Bank Act, by the Federal Home Loan Bank Board (acting directly or through the Federal Savings and Loan Insurance Corporation), in the case of any institution subject to any of those provisions.

"(3) The Federal Credit Union Act, by the Administrator of the National Credit Union Administration with respect to any Federal Credit Union.

"(4) The Acts to regulate commerce, by the Interstate Commerce Commission with respect to any common carrier subject to those Acts.

"(5) The Federal Aviation Act of 1958, by the Civil Aeronautics Board with respect to any air carrier or foreign air carrier subject to that Act.

"(6) The Packers and Stockyards Act, 1921 (except as provided in section 406 of that Act), by the Secretary of Agriculture with respect to any activities subject to that Act.

"(7) The Farm Credit Act of 1971, by the Farm Credit Administration with respect to any Federal land bank, Federal land bank association, Federal intermediate credit bank, and production credit association;

"(8) The Securities Exchange Act of 1934 by the Securities and Exchange Commission with respect to brokers and dealers; and

"(9) The Small Business Investment Act of 1958, by the Small Business Ad-Business Administration, with respect to small business investment companies.

"(b) For the purpose of the exercise by any agency referred to in subsection (a) of its powers under any Act referred to in that subsection, a violation of any requirement imposed under this title shall be deemed to be a violation of a requirement imposed under that Act. In addition to its powers under any provision of law specifically referred to in subsection (a), each of the agencies referred to in that subsection may exercise for the purpose of enforcing compliance with any requirement imposed under this title, any other authority conferred on it by law. The exercise of the authorities of any of the agencies referred to in subsection (a) for the purpose of enforcing compliance with any requirement imposed under this title shall in no way preclude the exercise of such authorities for the purpose of enforcing compliance with any other provision of law not relating to the prohibition of discrimination on the basis of sex or marital status with respect to any aspect of a credit transaction.

"(c) Except to the extent that enforcement of the requirements imposed under this title is specifically committed to some other Government agency under subsection (a), the Federal Trade Commission shall enforce such requirements. For the purpose of the exercise by the Federal Trade Commission of its functions and powers under the Federal Trade Commission Act, a violation of any requirement imposed under this title shall be deemed a violation of a requirement imposed under that Act. All of the functions and powers of the Federal Trade Commission under the Federal Trade Commission Act are available to the Commission to enforce compliance by any person with the requirements imposed under this title, irrespective of whether that person is engaged in commerce or meets any other jurisdictional tests in the Federal Trade Commission Act.

"(d) The authority of the Board to issue regulations under this title does not impair the authority of any other agency designated in this section to make rules respecting its own procedures in enforcing compliance with requirements imposed under this title.

"Sec. 705. Relation to State laws

"(a) A request for the signature of both parties to a marriage for the purpose of creating a valid lien, passing clear title, waiving inchoate rights to property, or assigning earnings, shall not constitute discrimination under this title: *Provided, however,* That this provision shall not be construed to permit a creditor to take sex or marital status into account in connection with the evaluation of creditworthiness of any applicant.

"(b) Consideration or application of State property laws directly or indirectly affecting creditworthiness shall not constitute discrimination for purposes of this title.

"(c) Any provision of State law which prohibits the separate extension of consumer credit to each party to a marriage shall not apply in any case where each party to a marriage voluntarily applies for separate credit from the same creditor: *Provided,* That in any case where such a State law is so preempted, each party to the marriage shall be solely responsible for the debt so contracted.

"(d) When each party to a marriage separately and voluntarily applies for and obtains separate credit accounts with the same creditor, those accounts shall not be aggregated or otherwise combined for purposes of determining permissible finance charges or permissible loan ceilings under the laws of any State or of the United States.

"(e) Except as otherwise provided in this title, the applicant shall have the option of pursuing remedies under the provisions of this title in lieu of, but not in addition to, the remedies provided by the laws of any State or governmental subdivision relating to the prohibition of discrimination on the basis of sex or marital status with respect to any aspect of a credit transaction.

"Sec. 706. Civil liability

"(a) Any creditor who fails to comply with any requirement imposed under this title shall be liable to the aggrieved applicant in an amount equal to the sum of any actual damages sustained by such applicant acting either in an individual capacity or as a representative of a class.

"(b) Any creditor who fails to comply with any requirement imposed under this title shall be liable to the aggrieved applicant for punitive damages in an amount not greater than $10,000, as determined by the court, in addition to any actual damages provided in section 706 (1): *Provided, however,* That in pursuing the recovery allowed under this subsection, the applicant may proceed only in an individual capacity and not as a representative of a class.

"(c) Section 706 (b) notwithstanding, any creditor who fails to comply with any requirement imposed under this title may be liable for punitive damages in the case of a class action in such amount as the court may allow, except that as to each member of the class no minimum recovery shall be applicable, and the total recovery in such action shall not exceed the lesser of $100,000 or 1 percent of the net worth of the creditor. In determining the amount of award in any class action, the court shall consider, among other relevant factors, the amount of any actual damages awarded, the frequency and persistence of failures of compliance by the creditor, the resources of the creditor, the number of persons adversely affected, and the extent to which the creditor's failure of compliance was intentional.

"(d) When a creditor fails to comply with any requirement imposed under this title, an aggrieved applicant may institute a civil action for preventive relief, including an application for a permanent or temporary injunction, restraining order, or other action.

"(e) In the case of any successful action to enforce the foregoing liability, the costs of the action, together with a reasonable attorney's fee as determined by the court shall be added to any damages awarded by the court under the provisions of subsections (a), (b), and (c) of this section.

"(f) No provision of this title imposing any liability shall apply to any act done or omitted in good faith in conformity with any rule, regulation, or interpretation thereof by the Board, notwithstanding that after such act or omission has occurred, such rule, regulation, or interpretation is amended, rescinded, or determined by judicial or other authority to be invalid for any reason.

"(g) Without regard to the amount in controversy, any action under this title may be brought in any United States district court, or in any other court of competent jurisdiction, within one year from the date of the occurrence of the violation.

SOME ADDRESSES...

FRAUD AND THEFT INFORMATION BUREAU
217 N. Seacrest Blvd.
Box 400
Boynton Beach, FL 33425

Publishes the BIN directory as well as a good newsletter.

BANKCARD HOLDERS OF AMERICA
333 Pennsylvania Ave, S.E.
Washington, D.C, 20003

Non-profit, "best" lists plus newsletter.

CONSUMER CREDIT CARD RAtING SERVICE
POB 5219
Santa Monica, CA 90405

Top 350 card poster plus newsletter for those in the business.

BANK CREDIT CARD OBSERVER
120 Wood Ave S.
Iselin, NJ 08830

CREDIT WORLD
243 N. Lindbergh Blvd.
St. Louis, MO 27357

Newsletter/magazine on credit business.